D1606546

Gerd Kerkhoff

Global Sourcing

Gerd Kerkhoff

Global Sourcing

*Opportunities for the Future
China, India, Eastern Europe –
How to Benefit from the
Potential of International
Procurement*

**WILEY-
VCH**

WILEY-VCH Verlag GmbH & Co. KGaA

Library of Congress Card No.:
applied for

British Library Cataloguing-in-Publication Data
A catalogue record for this book is available from the British Library.

Bibliographic information published by Die Deutsche Bibliothek
Die Deutsche Bibliothek lists this publication in the Deutsche Nationalbibliografie; detailed bibliograpic data is available in the Internet at <http://dnb.ddb.de>.

Typesetting Typomedia GmbH, Ostfildern
Printing and Binding Ebner & Spiegel GmbH, Ulm

Printed in the Federal Republic of Germany

Printed on acid-free paper

ISBN-13: 978-3-527-50232-5
ISBN-10: 3-527-50232-7

Table of Contents

Global Sourcing. Gerd Kerkhoff
Copyright © 2006 WILEY-VCH Verlag GmbH & Co. KGaA, Weinheim
ISBN: 3-527-50232-7

Foreword

Business failures and mass dismissals continue to make headlines. At the same time, cut-throat competition to win over customers is forcing companies to undertake substantial cost-cutting measures. Profits have been reduced to a bare minimum – often, even rendered entirely impossible. While an end to this development is not foreseeable in the near future, often the possibilities of actively steering against it are already exhausted. The potential of rationalization is largely tapped out, and any further cuts in the workforce could possibly lead to a shortage of capacity and the loss of know-how and quality. No business enterprise can or should deal with this against the background of rapidly increasing international competition.

An opportunity to stand one's ground in the face of these challenges and to bring in satisfactory returns and profitable growth, despite the enormous weight of the competition, is global sourcing. By this, I mean strategic international procurement. Through this kind of procurement on a global level, costs can be reduced by as much as 30% to 40% on average for many products and services. This cost reduction has a direct bearing on the bottom line of the enterprise. In many cases, the cost-cutting potential is in fact much higher. All this is achieved without having to compromise on the quality of the products by using alleged »cheap goods«. The qualifications and achievement potential of suppliers in China, India, and Eastern Europe are, in many cases, no longer inferior to the capabilities of Western companies.

It may well be known that because of these very reasons, leading international manufacturers of branded goods have long since been sourcing abroad. Nevertheless, I would like to illustrate, with the help of convincing examples, the significant part of global sourcing in the relentless rise of Adidas and other organizations. The strategy

Global Sourcing. Gerd Kerkhoff
Copyright © 2006 WILEY-VCH Verlag GmbH & Co. KGaA, Weinheim
ISBN: 3-527-50232-7

is not reserved for just this showcase enterprise. Many companies, regardless of their size and industry sector, are already profiting from global sourcing and are giving their earnings the much-needed thrust, even in economically challenging times. International procurement is in fact increasingly acting as the sheet anchor for economically hit companies. Credit institutes award plus points for the consistent use of international procurement when rating business enterprises.

Global sourcing cannot, however, be implemented in a flash. The new strategy demands a fundamental rethinking in the purchasing departments, which even today in many cases are limited to working with suppliers situated in the immediate vicinity. Furthermore, some organizational measures and meticulous market analyses are required. This initial investment of time and effort should not, however, deter you from making your purchasing department a significant profit booster of your company.

This book shows how earning potential that has been lying dormant until now can be unleashed through global sourcing. It is not about highlighting the efficiency of the instrument with the help of possibly complicated business management formulae. The focus of *Global Sourcing Opportunities for the Future* is to impart tangible benefits that can be directly implemented in practice. At the same time, this book also attempts to show that the often criticized phenomenon of globalization, which opened up the way for global sourcing, need not, as a rule, contribute to unemployment in the industrialized countries. On the contrary, it helps Western companies to stay competitive in the international market and contributes to protect jobs that are in danger in the local markets. Many of our clients have succeeded in providing an increased number of jobs by implementing global sourcing.

Needless to say, I am not an outright advocate of globalization and its consequences. I am completely aware that this process includes developments that could lead to social hardships and other adverse economic effects in some regions. However, I shall not go into these details in this book. I am going to concentrate exclusively on the unique opportunities global sourcing offers to future-oriented business enterprises. Besides, I would like to encourage the concerned managers to exploit the possibilities of global sourcing that would help them act in an entrepreneurial and responsible manner within the confines of the political framework. After all, the procurement of cost-effective raw material and services abroad is a decisively contributing factor in sustaining the price competitiveness of local products in the global market.

I would like to thank our clients, our contacts at the credit institutes, and my colleagues for their active support with the work of this book. Particularly, I would like to mention my partners Marc Kloepfel, Ralph Markert, Christian Michalak, Dr. Ralph Niederdrenk, and Dirk Schäfer, who with their know-how and long-standing practical experience have been major contributors to the outcome of this book. I also thank the law firm, Blasius & Kollegen for their pragmatic contribution to the subject »Legal Aspects of Global Sourcing«. Further, the following book would not have been possible without the exceptional assistance of Yurda Yilmaz and my three Senior Area Managers Seoul Min, Parwis Masomi and Duran Sarikaya. A special thank-you goes to my wife Stefanie, whose encouragement helped me realize this book. My conversations with her and her suggestions have helped me immensely throughout.

Düsseldorf, Germany, May 2006   *Gerd Kerkhoff*

Chapter 1
A World without Borders

Globalization. Almost no other term divides the world today so intensely. Staunch supporters of this development speak of a new era of growth and prosperity. One of the advocates of globalization is Bill Gates, chairman of Microsoft, Inc. He believes that »This is a very exciting time in the world of information. It's not just that the personal computer has come along as a great tool. The whole pace of business is moving faster. Globalization is forcing companies to do things in new ways.« In the Western world, people have to put an end to resisting the laws of globalization and stop pretending as though these laws do not apply to them. Kofi Annan, Secretary General of the United Nations has remarked: »It has been said that arguing against globalization is like arguing against the laws of gravity.« It is therefore clear that the effects of globalization are inevitable and that we must change now or be left out.

Vehement critics warn of an undue advantage of multinational concerns, which could have disastrous effects on the situation in the Third World countries, employment in the industrial nations, and further development of democracy. Prof. Dr. Hab A. Bien, professor of Finance at the University of Warsaw, Poland, defines globalization and its consequences with the following words: »Globalization is making the world visibly smaller; that which is distant is getting easier to reach. At the same time, the world is expanding because we are still not able to look over far-off horizons.« A seemingly simple yet appropriate explanation, which is, moreover, marked by optimism.

In the past, there have always been equally controversial discussions about fundamental political, economic, and social changes. The debate in the 1950s about the pros and cons of atomic energy is just one example. The following two decades were marked by debates about the positive and negative effects of industrial society.

Global Sourcing. Gerd Kerkhoff
Copyright © 2006 WILEY-VCH Verlag GmbH & Co. KGaA, Weinheim
ISBN: 3-527-50232-7

The »risk society« was the focus of the 1980s. Finally, a decade later, the term globalization emerged – with widely varying interpretations about the possible repercussions. Such manner of interpretations is inevitable for a new trend. In an interview for Asia Society Online, world-famous economist and Nobel Laurette, Amartya Sen, said, »Economic globalization itself could be a source of major advancement of living conditions, and it often is. The main difficulty is that the circumstances in which it produces the maximum benefits for poorer people do not exist now. This is not however an argument for being against global economic contact but rather an argument for working towards a better division of benefits from global economic contact.«

Globalization does not stand for a completely new development. The quest to cross boundaries, to learn new things and to profit from them runs like a common thread throughout history. Initially, the focus was on tapping new sources of raw material in distant lands. Later, traders set out to procure high-quality goods abroad, which when sold in the home country realized hefty profits. In the recent past (i. e. in the era of globalization), countries aim their transnational activities mainly to develop new markets for their own products and services. Increasingly, however, the focus has been on procuring individual parts or complete systems in countries that have attractive labor costs and moreover, that offer good quality.

In the past, the term globalization not only describe initiatives and developments that would lead to a sustainable boost in the turnover and profits of business enterprises, but also would open new horizons and provide new insights to the people. It also stood for the calamitous quest of many politicians to expand their sphere of control in other countries. The world wars of the 20th century are perfect examples of that.

Politics charts the path

The current trend of globalization was recognizable in Western Europe and the US for the first time after the end of the Second World War. Development aid emerged, colonies were granted independence, multinational companies were established and the consumer-oriented society led to ever-increasing demands by the consumers. Gradually the governments decided to work together and cooperate on activities that were hitherto carried out alone. In this way, in 1951 the European Coal and Steel Community (ECSC) was founded with the member states Belgium, Germany, Luxembourg, France, Italy, and the Netherlands. This gave the authority to make decisions about the coal and steel industry in these countries to a supranational body – the »High Authority.« The founding of the Council of Europe in 1949 led to the emergence of a community of European countries with the task of promoting economic and social progress in the member states. In 1957, six countries founded the European Economic Commission (EEC) – the forerunner to the European Union (EU) that was founded in 1992. Today, the tasks of the EU go much beyond trade and the economy. In »Europe with virtually no borders«, the tasks have spilled over to ensuring civil rights, environmental protection and regional development.

The opening-up of individual countries has been gradual and restricted to the Western world. Almost everyone can recall how, until just a few years ago, the Warsaw Pact countries under the leadership of the Soviet Union (USSR) were reckoned to be the greatest threat to the Western nations. Similarly many people saw the developments in communist China with much suspicion. Both regions strictly isolated themselves and their citizens from the West. Their political activities and strategies were considered to be largely uncertain.

Everything, though, has changed in the last few years. The USSR collapsed in 1991, as the member states of the Warsaw Pact declared their independence and opened their borders to the Western world. Today, it is a matter of course that, for example, the American and the Russian President meet each other in a completely friendly setting. This has been possible only because both sides wish to profit from cross-border cooperation. Since 2004, Estonia, Latvia, Lithuania, Poland, Slovakia, Slovenia, the Czech Republic, and Hungary are a part of the European Union (EU). Many other countries of the former »Eastern Bloc« are interested in joining the EU as soon as possible. The borders within Europe are being blurred out at a rapid pace, thus helping the development of a broad foundation that ensures peace across countries and creates prosperity amongst the member states.

The state visit of the former US President Richard Nixon to China in 1972 led to the first opening-up of the country and its population, which now stands at almost 1.3 billion people. Ever since, the People's Republic has rapidly developed into a country that not only seeks international contacts, but also receives offers from almost all governments and large companies. Here, too, the walls have long since crumbled. The age of isolation is long gone. Global cooperation is the order of the day. Clearly a development that, no one would have dared to predict some years ago.

India, too, has made an about-turn in the recent past – from a state-controlled, regimented economy, influenced by socialism to a social market economy. Since this new orientation and the opening of the economy to foreign companies, the nation's economic growth rate has been steadily surging upwards. According to forecasts made by the renowned investment bank Goldman Sachs, the Indian economy will be the third largest in the world by 2050. This development will not be driven just by the rising production within the country but also because India is slowly remerging the most attractive market for domestic and foreign products.

This is how even countries that were looked upon with distrust in the past are erasing their borders. Globalization paves the way for long-term peace and a cooperative partnership beyond national borders.

Dynamic development processes in the economy

Globalization of the economy has been decisively influenced by politics. On July 22, 1944, while the Second World War was still in progress, a stable monetary system was decided upon at the legendary conference in Bretton Woods in America. With this step, international trade that used fixed exchange rates determined by the US dollar (the key currency), would have been free from trade barriers. However, the system failed. Nevertheless, the World Bank and International Monetary Fund (which were also founded in 1944) continued to function. The General Agreement on Tariffs and Trade (GATT) emerged three years later. After several rounds of negotiations, tariffs and other trade restraints were gradually abolished. At the end of the last GATT round on April 15, 1994, the World Trade Organization (WTO) was founded. Today, some 150 countries, which generate over 90% of the volume of world trade, are affiliated to the WTO and are committed to observing the basic rules of WTO in their foreign trade relations. One of these rules is the commitment to deal with foreign products, services and their suppliers, just as one would deal with the domestic ones.

Free trade, however, also poses great challenges to the domestic industry. European textile manufacturers, for example, have to come to terms with the fact that with effect from January 1, 2005, import quotas (which so far have been in existence) have now been struck off without any substitution. With this elimination of import quotas, the sector is living through the worst upheaval in its history. China is the country benefiting from this new regulation. Today, around 25% of the global garment imports come from China. Many observers believe that China shall quickly develop into the »tailor of the world«. The World Bank also endorses this prediction. It anticipates that Chinese textile exports to Europe shall double within a very short time. The bankers will be justified in their estimate, since large chains particularly are increasingly stocking their shelves with affordable goods from China or they are manufacturing their products in China. All for a good reason: The hourly wages for seamstresses in China are clearly under 1 US dollar, and the quality is comparable to that of the West.

The Chinese, though, are not willing to simply settle for supplying affordable goods to their foreign customers. Large business enterprises in the country are literally going on a global shopping spree, looking to buy into well-known Western concerns. Early in 2005, Shanghai Automotive planned a 1.4 billion euros entry into the British MG Rover Group, but aborted the negotiations in April 2005 following the negative due diligence report. In 2004, the computer manufacturer Lenovo took over the PC division of IBM for an equally high sum. The appetite of the Chinese to buy existing companies abroad is steadily increasing: China spent 340 million US dollars in acquiring international companies in the year 2000 alone. Straszheim Global Advisors (who specialize in China) forecast that if this trend continues then in 2005 China will be spending approximately 14 billion US dollars taking over European companies.

Investors from the Far East are not interested in buying only large, renowned companies. Increasingly, medium-sized businesses also feature on the list. The goal of these actions is extremely ambitious: the Chinese wish to make their companies into global brands as quickly as possible. By buying well-known brands, they are achieving a global presence in the shortest time and gaining the technological know-how that their own companies still frequently lack.

A whole lot of other countries that were of little economic significance are also experiencing dynamic development processes. Noteworthy among these (besides those in Eastern Europe), are the industrial countries of East Asia like Singapore, Hong Kong, Taiwan and South Korea. These so-called Tiger states experienced an extraordinary boom in the last 30 years. Earlier, Singapore belonged to the poorer countries where almost exclusively cheap goods that did not have to meet any high quality standards were manufactured. Today it ranks among the most important financial services centers of the world and is one of the metropolitan centers of international knowledge transfer. In the meantime, Malaysia, Thailand, the Philippines and Indonesia have also developed into industrial climbers and also belong to the group of Tiger states.

Essentially, by focusing on core competencies, certain countries have succeeded in becoming booming regions. India and increasingly South Africa, for example, specialize in Business Process Outsourcing (BPO) i. e. carrying out IT-enabled services (ITES) for local and foreign companies. India also offers global customer service through call centers. It is not just large international banks that are increasingly availing of such services and profiting from India's highly qualified albeit low-wage personnel. The opportunities for cost-cutting are enormous. An Indian call center employee, with his average annual earnings of 3,600 euros, earns only a fifth of what his counterpart in Great Britain would earn. The British HSBC, the world's second largest credit institute, reports that every job that is outsourced to a low-wage country is able to save the company more than 15,000 euros annually, without compromising on the customer service. Therefore, the bank plans to double the number of its employees in Asia in the foreseeable future. Currently, Deutsche Bank partially processes its electronic funds transfer in Bangalore, India.

China is not leading only in the textile sector, where it has already overtaken Turkey. Buyers of »C-parts« i. e. products with a low purchase price, are sure to find a plethora of Chinese manufacturers who are able to submit very attractive offers. The same applies to shoes. Italy has long since lost its position as the Mecca for buyers of the shoe store chains. Every second pair on the store shelves is imported from China.

In the last few years, Eastern European companies have earned an excellent reputation as suppliers to the automobile industry and no longer need to dread the comparison with the West in terms of quality. Not to mention the significantly lower labor costs that gives them an edge over the competition. An example furnished by the consulting firm McKinsey documents the economic efficiency of procuring components overseas and of establishing international production facilities. According to this, a manufacturer of basic automobile gearboxes saves approximately 250 euros per gearbox – inclusive of custom duty and transportation costs – by procuring the most valuable components in the Czech Republic and by finishing the production of the systems, which are meant for the Chinese and Mexican markets, in these two countries itself.

Trade has helped the European Union establish closer links with its immediate neighbors. In the first place, the Union has stepped up its trade with the candidate countries of central and Eastern Europe that are due to join the EU. The agreements with these countries, known as »Europe agreements«, are intended to promote and catapult free trade between them and the EU before they actually join. All these countries are, even today, among the most significant trade partners of the EU economy, and it is foreseeable that this relationship will further intensify.

In 2002, China was fourth on the list of EU's main import countries, close on the heels of Switzerland and Japan. Chinese companies exported goods worth over 81 billion euros to the EU. Meanwhile, China earned the sixth position in the list of EU's main export countries by importing goods worth 34 billion euros.

Countries are increasingly taking the initiative to set the course for sustainable economic growth thus helping their citizens prosper. The Director of Innovation Transfer Center of Poland, Mrs. Helena Korolewska-Mroz remarked: »An unbelievable dynamic exists in many countries. Countries that were not too long ago regarded as developing countries will catapult themselves, in the span of a single generation, into the sphere of leading nations of the 21st century. Bold visions for the future are being framed and implemented there.« Simultaneously, there is another development process underway that supports the boom in these regions. For instance, the erstwhile industrialized countries after reaching a stage of maturity are now focusing on services and undertaking production of technically complex products to satisfy the ever-increasing needs of their people while the less challenging jobs are being relocated abroad.

Significant changes in society

The trend towards globalization is also reflected through significant changes in society. For example, mobility of the people is increasing at a rapid pace since many years. The number of passenger kilometers in international air traffic has risen more than a hundred times since 1950. Cross-border rail and road traffic too, is dynamically increasing. People are no longer vacationing exclusively within their own country. Long-distance trips are in vogue. Reasonably priced holiday packages are alluring people to make short visits to neighboring countries. For many, business trips to China, India or some other country are already part of the everyday business life. It is no longer something extraordinary to take semesters abroad, not only to profit from the know-how of the respective country but also to get to know the different mentality of the people. And this not only apply to the new generation from the industrialized countries. Today, Eastern Europeans and Asians are studying at international elite universities as much as prospective engineers and businessmen from the countries of the West. Mobility, however, is not restricted simply to vacation travel and studying abroad. Decolonization has led to people from the former colonies returning in hordes to their colonial states. Western cities have become multicultural centers. Paris, London, and New York are examples of metropolitan cities that have an above-average share of international population. It is not just in these cities, however, that elements of diverse cultures are part of the urban landscape. In most industrialized nations today, people do not raise an eyebrow when they see Chinese or Italian restaurants. Bars and pubs playing African music are no longer uncommon. The reverse however, also holds true. Home specialties can be purchased at many places all over the world, and one can also visit restaurants with local cuisine abroad.

Meanwhile, Western consumer goods have conquered the entire world. The spread of television, the increase in consumer advertising and the increasing number of international films have enormously contributed to this end. Today, no matter in which country one lives, everyone knows blue jeans and Coca-Cola as well as McDonald's, which began its triumphant success outside North America in 1971.

The Internet has developed into a significant global source of information for individuals and companies. The number of Internet connections continues to increase at a rapid pace. With this, small and medium-sized businesses as well as less-developed countries have access to information that until now could only be generated by incurring high costs. At the same time, price comparisons and financial transactions are possible in seconds. This increased transparency and the exchange of data at lightning speed also leads to clearly intensified competition among the suppliers. Nevertheless, no country can afford to isolate itself from global markets in the future. This is because in almost all countries globalization has led to a noticeable improvement in the living conditions. Regions that took an aggressive stance against other countries to the challenges posed by the opening of the markets were the ones that registered the biggest successes. Use the example of East Asia – only four decades ago, almost the entire area was among the poorest regions of the world. With the first few steps towards globalization, the standard of living of the population started improving continuously. Democracy set in slowly but steadily. The economy showed a positive development. Topics like environmental protection and improvement of working conditions continued to gain importance.

A comparison of the anticipated development of the world population up to the year 2050 proves just how important the consistent development of globalization is for the Western economy. It is, in fact, almost vital for its survival. According to this forecast, the world population will increase from the current 6.5 billion to about 9.1 billion. The growth, according to the United Nations, will stem mostly from Asia (+44%), Africa (+140%) and Latin America (+51%). In Europe, on the other hand, the population will reduce by 17%. A disproportionate growth in turnover is expected mainly outside Europe in the long run.

Germany: Example of a Western Economy slowly adapting to globalization

Like many developing countries today, Germany and the other European countries received massive aid from the US after the Second World War. The European Recovery Program (initiated by the then US foreign minister George E. Marshall) was aimed at helping regions that were marked as severely hit, to stand on their feet once again and to prevent communism from spreading in these countries. 16 European countries participated in the so-called Marshall Plan Conference in July 1947. The Eastern European countries were also invited; however, the USSR strictly forbade them to participate. Goods, raw material, foodstuff, and credit worth 1.5 billion US dollars flowed into West Germany between 1948 and 1952 and provided many areas with the foundation to make a new beginning. Among these were mainly coal mining and the power industry.

Right from the start, the then German Chancellor Konrad Adenauer directed his foreign policy strictly to become a reliable partner of the West through a multitude of contracts and agreements. For him, the guarantee of freedom by integrating with the West held a much higher position than the pursuit for reunification. In the following years, the cooperation with the neighboring countries towards the West and the US was continuously developed and laid on a solid foundation, for example, first with the European Coal and Steel Community and then with accession into the EEC. Only after the fall of the Berlin Wall in 1989 and the collapse of the Soviet Union did Germany begin opening towards the East. Up until then, political and economic contacts with Eastern Europe had more of a scarcity value. Today, guests of state from these countries are received just as warmly as guests from any other country. Globalization has in this way also found its way into German politics.

Germany continues to be the world's most prolific exporting nation. In 2004 alone, German companies exported goods worth approximately 728 billion euros, thus taking the export surplus to a record 156 billion euros. This is proof enough that foreign trade has become the central pillar of the German economy. Even the Federation of German Wholesale and Foreign Trade (BGA) endorse this assessment. The BGA is convinced that the expansion of the EU, coupled with the economic growth in the emerging economies, opens up markets with a high growth potential in the long term, and are therefore causes for optimism.

It is however quite clear that Germany can, by no means, maintain its enviable position at the top in all areas. The textile industry, for example, has to struggle to survive against the stiff competition from China and Turkey. The leather goods industry (which has downsized its workforce by 90% since the early 1970s) is also facing difficult times. Meanwhile, the production has been moved almost entirely to the economically viable countries, leaving only about 4,000 people employed in the leather goods sector in Germany. A similar trend is seen with the automobile spare parts suppliers and many other companies that have also shifted to low-wage countries that are attractive not only because of low manufacturing costs of C-parts but also for the good quality of their products. Manufacturing costs even in the countries that are generally believed to be expensive are much more competitive than those in Germany. A good example is the power saw manufacturer Stihl, which by manufacturing in Switzerland, saves 30% per hour as compared to the production in Germany. Costs in the US are 44% below the German average whereas the difference in costs between Germany and Brazil is a massive 86%.

The state-aided mineral coal industries, steel and chemical sectors are also in a very precarious position. Foreign competitors with innovative ideas and efficient products have long since overtaken the German companies. In Germany, future industries like gene technology are to a large extent underdeveloped. Likewise, the expansive pharmaceutical industry has almost completely moved out of Germany. Even German banks and large service providers are seriously considering the prospect of relocating their head offices or at least important departments abroad. The situation is such that it makes no difference that the German Minister for Economic Affairs is asking for »modern patriotism« and is exhorting the entrepreneurs to remain in Germany. Extremely high labor costs and tax rates, which are much higher than in other countries, curb the interest to support production in Germany in a sustainable manner. Those who do not venture into foreign markets and continue to create value for their company exclusively in Germany run the risk of losing out to the ever-intensifying international competition, at least in the medium term.

The label »Made in Germany«, which significantly contributed to the success of German products globally, is now convincing fewer buyers. No wonder that reports about grave defects in the quality of high-end German brands are increasingly making the headlines. For example, in 2004, Daimler-Chrysler had to call back limousines of the A, E and S classes, as well as from the model series CL and CLK because of grave defects in the electronic hydraulics system. As a result the luxury automobile manufacturer had to be content with the third-last place in a customer satisfaction analysis conducted by the Germany automobile club. Foreign brands that were looked upon as qualitatively inferior a few years ago, stood far ahead of Daimler-Chrysler.

Siemens, too, had to see its image being marred. Apart from the problems with the software of a new cellular phone model, the electronic giant had to admit to serious defects in its low-floor streetcar »Combino« in the recent past. The list of such examples can go on. Foreign manufacturers like Toyota are profiting from these developments and continue to register immense sales successes all over Germany. With that, globalization is reaching new dimensions for the German economy. *Spiegel*, the leading German news magazine, therefore reports »Bye-bye ›Made in Germany‹« and the *Handelsblatt*, a leading German economics newspaper says, »Something is very wrong with ›Made in Germany‹.« What matters most is the convincing power of the brand and not the country in which the goods are produced.

Meanwhile, even the most traditional German companies are discovering this change. For example, Miele now manufactures its household appliances in the Czech Republic. Engineering and plant construction, the most important sector for increasing turnover in the German economy, is planning at least a partial farewell from German production facilities by the end of this decade. According to a survey conducted by the consulting firm Roland Berger, 90% of the companies in this segment want to relocate parts of their production abroad in the near future. The picture in the automobile spare parts industry also looks similar. The accounting and consulting firm Ernst & Young reports, »Every second German automobile spare parts supplier is currently planning to construct production facilities in Eastern Europe or China.« It is by no means only the favorable labor and manufacturing costs of the new locations that the companies hold so dear. Highly qualified employees, flexibility in the factor of work and the work habits are equally important reasons for the scheduled relocation. »Meanwhile, there are excellent engineers in Beijing and Bratislava, too,« says Peter Fuß, head of the automotive department at Ernst & Young. The expert in this segment opines that even regions like Southeast Asia, South America, and India will develop into similarly attractive manufacturing locations for German automobile spare parts suppliers. Fuß declares, »Germany as the automobile manufacturing location is in complete danger.«

The increasing export of work, however, is creating new jobs in Germany. In fact, more jobs are being created than being lost in the country. This result, which is surprising at first glance, is backed by the study »Effects of Globalization on Employment«, published by the Federal Ministry of Finance in 2004. The Ministry provides the reasons for and refers to the development of the contribution of foreign economics in the Gross Domestic Product. It arises from the difference between exports and imports. Taking inflation into account, this so-called trade balance has increased five times between 1991 and 2003. Currently, a good one-fifth of the domestic value added and with it the number of jobs depends on exports – and in an increasing trend. According to the interpretation of the Federal Ministry of Finance, this means »nothing other than the fact that Germany is utilizing the strengthened international division of labor, including the relocation of production and the advance imports in order to ensure domestic jobs and to create new jobs in the process of the structural change.«

Mr. Ireneusz Gorecki, managing director of GB Resources Polska has reached the conclusion that »the growing internationalization of the German economy is opening up many opportunities for more jobs in the country«. Simple, labor-intensive activities would be relocated abroad and this would at the same time spur on the development and production of specialized high-value goods. The study however complains »that many established companies do not utilize the potential of global production networks actively enough and as a result leave the growth potential untapped«.

Large backlog in Western society

It is natural to expect a certain degree of openness towards other countries from Western nations that pride themselves on being world champions in exports. However, that is not so. Among many sections of the population, there continue to exist mental blocks against nations that have long since developed into important trade partners. For example some people still deride the Chinese to be »dog eaters«. Poles and other Eastern Europeans are looked down upon as notorious thieves. Many critics qualify India as being filthy, without having visited the country even once. And a propensity to violence is attached to the South Americans.

Everything that does not come from the West is often met with skepticism. All this, despite the fact that Eastern Europe, the former Soviet Union, and China have taken big steps to draw themselves nearer to Western customs and that, exactly like the Western world, they are concerned about the prosperity of their citizens. Therefore a rethinking is urgently required. The American economy and many European neighbors have long since grasped this development and are working open-mindedly with companies from all over the world. Companies need to emulate these examples without fail if they do not wish to miss the boat in the medium term.

The prejudices against countries, that one is not completely familiar with reflect even in the planning of vacations overseas. Germans and the British travel to Majorca and the Canary Islands with pleasure. The Americans and the French prefer to stay in their home countries. This is not just because the journey lasts just a couple of hours and because airlines and travel agencies constantly offer very attractive, cheap deals. The reason is very often something else. In these countries, the vacationers can be sure of getting exactly what they get back home. And lastly, the Western tourists also find it extremely attractive to be able to speak in their own language to the hotel and inn personnel.

The reason is not just the aversion to learning another language. Many people think it only natural that every foreigner who might be interested in conducting business with them should master either the native language or at least English – a demand that in these times of global markets is arrogant and does not particularly contribute to promoting the reputation of one's country as a cosmopolitan one. It is only gradually that young Western managers and engineers are recognizing the importance of knowledge of foreign languages for their career and for the international success of their employers. Personnel consultants continue to be posed with a very challenging task when recruiting Western candidates for foreign assignments. Such recruitments are still not too difficult to manage if the positions are in the US or in other Western countries. If, however, the position to be filled is in China, India, or in some other part of the world, it tests the persuasive skills of the consultant to the fullest and also requires a proper »compensation for pain and suffering« in the form of clear allowances in the salary. The necessity of globalization and the readiness to participate actively in its development has not yet caught on in the minds of many Europeans.

However, when it comes to profiting, no one wants to miss the opportunity. »Smart shopping« (i.e., the hunt for bargains) has become the nation's favorite sport. Hopefully, this satisfaction at landing a great buy will promote the readiness to show some openness towards other countries and their people.

Globalization cannot be held back any more

Even the most vehement opponents of globalization have to realize at some point, that globalization is like a law of nature. The Western economies can only survive if they rise to the challenge and if they consistently use the advantages of global integration. The protectionism of the last few years cannot be sustained any longer if one wants to be a part of the forecasted development of the world economy. After all, it has long been proven that the international exchange of goods leads to the prosperity of all those involved. Through the intensified international division of labor, salaries in the low-wage countries increase. In regions where innovative and complex capital and consumer goods of high quality are manufactured, the income situation and the quality of life, both improve in a sustainable manner. There is therefore, no reason to whine about the international markets growing together. On the contrary, we should be happy that globalization presents us with the unique opportunity to strengthen the global economy and to ensure peace.

From an economic perspective, it makes no sense to obstinately latch on to local sectors that were once economic »pearls« but that have lost their shine lately. In Western countries, sectors that have not made a noteworthy contribution to the Gross Domestic Product since long are kept alive with the help of enormous state subsidies. For example, there are enough companies abroad which can produce significantly and efficiently in the steel sector than is possible in Europe. Europeans should essentially concentrate on their core competencies like research and technology and procure simpler components abroad. The fact that active globalization can become a »job creator« for Western countries has already been proven by the Federal Ministry of Finance and universities in their studies.

Chapter 2
Global Sourcing – Procuring from all over the World

Presumably, everyone knows brands such as Nike, Adidas, or Puma. However, did you know that these successful companies manufacture their products almost exclusively abroad i. e. that they outsource important parts of the value addition to international suppliers? Only design and marketing are largely predetermined by the company headquarters. Sales are also the responsibility of service providers. However, the three giants in the sports goods sector are not exceptions. Other businesses in the garments industry or PC manufacturers also have their products manufactured to detailed specifications in low-wage countries – at sensationally favorable prices and in absolute top quality. The goods directly reach the shelves of global dealers, furnished with individual instructions for use in the respective countries. No wonder that Herbert Hainer, CEO and chairman of the executive board of Adidas AG, could once again announce a record result for the financial year 2005. The Adidas head states, »Our organization has registered a record turnover, and also record figures in gross earnings margin and profit.«

In these times of ever-increasing price and competition pressures, international procurement has become one of the most essential building blocks for the success of the showcase enterprises of Western countries. After all, favorable material costs are fast becoming the most important reason to have an international presence in procurement and, in this way, to ensure sustainable success. Temporary price promotions get the turnover moving only in the short term. The possibilities of reduction in costs are often already exhausted and further cost-cutting in the areas of personnel and production could inevitably lead to loss of quality and image. A disastrous combination indeed! Therefore, most company heads should become more active if they not only want to continue to differentiate themselves from the competition but also wish to drive

Global Sourcing. Gerd Kerkhoff
Copyright © 2006 WILEY-VCH Verlag GmbH & Co. KGaA, Weinheim
ISBN: 3-527-50232-7

profitable growth. The reduction of the degree of company-internal value added, as is noticeable in almost all sectors, leads to an automatic appreciation of the procurement management in companies. This should accompany the orientation of the purchasing organization to international sourcing markets.»Therefore, Dimitrij Asaturov, CEO of Holding LEDA is convinced, that often a purchase component of over 50% of the company's cost indicates the influence of professional procurement on company results. A strategic approach helps in avoiding common mistakes.«

Lee Scott, Wal-Mart's current CEO, and other top Wal-Mart executives make the point that Wal-Mart is serving American consumers by getting imported goods at the lowest possible prices. Some economists even credit Wal-Mart with lowering the US rate of inflation by its aggressive cost-cutting strategies while raising US productivity through its supply chain efficiencies. But when Lee Scott and Tom Schoewe, Wal-Mart's chief financial officer, talk with Wall Street analysts, they also point to global sourcing as vital for maintaining and increasing Wal-Mart's bottom-line profits.

However, the notion of looking for reliable suppliers beyond the region where the company headquarters is located has not yet caught on in most businesses. Japan is, even today, a world champion in exports but an amateur in imports. In the near future, Western companies will be judged by how well they amalgamate in the international sourcing markets, how they manage change and strive to transform themselves.

This advice applies, above all, to medium-sized companies. The experience of Kerkhoff Consulting shows that almost 80% of all small and medium-sized enterprises (SMEs) procure their goods and services from the area falling under their own zip code. The remaining (almost 20%) SMEs are also not convincing with their entrepreneurial foresight. These companies procure within a large fraction of their own country and, if they believe in being particularly progressive, in neighboring countries. In many cases, only a few dare to tread new paths in procurement by orienting themselves to the world market, offering favorable costs. Quite often, the reasons for such local patriotism have very little to do with management, because most businesses feel they are in very good hands with their suppliers from their neighborhood. They are not aware if these prices and services can really sustain with the competition. This is really surprising because consumers in Western Countries are getting more price-conscious when it comes to their personal sphere. After all, global sourcing does enable clear cost-cutting potential.

The European Union is a relatively open economy: international trade accounted for over 14% of its gross domestic product in 2000, compared with 12% for the United States and 11% for Japan. The EU is the world's biggest importer of goods from the 49 least developed countries. The import statistics have been constantly rising and will continue to do so. This development should be a warning signal for local suppliers. They have to react now and find convincing solutions to the attractive offers of the growing international competition. One can assume that companies that do not source globally henceforth will cease to be competitive in the next three to five years. They run the risk of becoming insolvent or of degenerating into takeover candidates.

Principally, the industry still does not have reason to panic. The former head of purchasing of Volkswagen, Dr. José Ignacio López de Arriortúa, convincingly proved that among most of the component suppliers, a large amount of untapped potential for improvement is waiting to be discovered. However, those who exclusively restrict themselves to complaining about globalization as being the gravedigger of the ancillary industry run the risk of soon steering their company into ruin.

Naturally, one should not conceal the fact that global sourcing is no miracle cure that can conjure up, with lightning speed, sparkling sources of profit for companies that are in the red or are posting lean profits. Those who are not well versed with the international market are at the risk of being shipwrecked, instead of being able to add new or additional brilliance to their balance sheet. International procurement can become the real profit driver only when the company works together with purchasing experts from the respective countries from which the company wishes to import. These experts know the conditions in their market up to the last detail and also know how best to react to the socio-cultural behavior patterns in their regions. Import/export traders, too, offer similar services. Whether this service is worth it or not, is debatable, because these service providers demand commission not just from the buyer, but also from the supplier.

Naturally, there are cases where, right from the very outset, global sourcing as a strategy for procurement does not even come into question, or in fact may be inefficient. This could apply in cases where the costs for international procurement, like additional quality checks, logistics, transport, or communication, exceed the value of the concerned product. Critical products that are extremely important for the production flow are, on the other hand, frequently very suitable for global sourcing. Corresponding (intermediate) storage provides the necessary prerequisites. This, then, is more a question of organization.

Growth-oriented companies in particular, not only use their global-sourcing activities to develop new sources of procurement but also to ensure their presence in the long term. One such company is, for example, the home-improvement chain Obi. The Obi team in the Eastern European countries conducted surveys and analyzed whether it would not perhaps be profitable to build a sales network. The result was clear. The first Obi market was established in Poland and others followed. In the middle term, the German market-sector leader wants to enter over a hundred markets in Eastern Europe and Russia and establish itself as the market leader.

What exactly is global sourcing?

Global sourcing is much more than mere inquiries for some requirements in countries with cheap raw material costs low labor costs. There is, however, no uniform definition. One may describe global sourcing as »the orientation of the procurement activities of companies to available sourcing markets worldwide«, »the strategic orientation of supply management towards utilizing global procurement sources«, or of the »systematic, cross-border procurement measures that are oriented to the global market«. Volkswagen takes the holistic perspective by describing global sourcing as »a continuous process for the planning, regulation, realization, and control of worldwide procurement activities, in order to improve the quality, service, and competitiveness of standard parts.« Europe's largest automobile manufacturer for standard parts has introduced global sourcing throughout the concern, to become competitive beyond the complete lifecycle of a product.

This makes it very clear: global sourcing is much more than just the extension of sourcing markets to other countries. Strategic global procurement does not just ensure the supply of necessary products and services. The knowledge of foreign markets and suppliers makes it possible to identify future developments well in time and to profit from them. It is a strategy that makes procurement a long-term profit-bringer for the company. In other words, those who conduct global sourcing prudently, invest in the continuous competitiveness of their companies.

Global sourcing is not about a short-term management trend that is initiated and marketed successfully by a more or less well-known management guru. Nor is it, as is frequently the case, just another success formula standing on a weak base. Global sourcing has a history going back centuries. Even in ancient times traders traveled on ship or rode pack animals to reach distant lands in order to procure there at favorable costs or to conquer the market there with their own goods. The Sumerians, for example, conducted booming trade with Egypt, Syria, and Asia Minor as early as the third century BC. In the days of the Roman Empire traders sold utensils, silver jewelry, or spices to the neighboring Germanic tribes. In the 16th century, and not just a few years ago, Asian markets were opened up for international trade. The Dutch East India Company was established then.

Right from the 14th century, trading families and their expansive companies started gaining in importance internationally. The Fugger dynasty was one of the most prominent and successful dynasties. This dynasty from Augsburg, Germany, maintained, as early as the mid-15th century, close business relations with Milan, Venice, London, and Antwerp. Thus, global sourcing was conducted centuries ago and led to the economic success of all those involved.

Those who believe the various reports will probably be convinced that China is the only country where global procurement is worthwhile. It is true that in the last few years this huge country has developed into a procurement paradise for all those who wish to restore their vertical range of manufacture to an efficient size, to procure individual parts or complete systems and assemblies abroad. This applies to the automobile industry just as much as to the areas of steel, machines, textiles, and shoes, or electronics. And these are just some examples. Just how attractive target-oriented procurement of certain materials is in defined markets, is explained in detail in this book.

Today it is a fact that no company, irrespective of its size, can afford to dispense with global sourcing if it does not wish to be relegated to the league of losers in the ever-intensifying international competition. Dr. Frank-J. Müssigbrodt, managing partner of the Network Corporate Finance GmbH & Co. KG, therefore, recommends: »The global dynamics of the sourcing markets will fundamentally change the supplier structure of successful medium-sized companies in the next few years. It is, therefore, important to act early, in order to guarantee competitive advantage.« The economy is growing closer together. The doors to the foreign sourcing markets are wide open. Entrepreneurs should make use of this unique opportunity and increase the profitability of their companies in a sustainable manner. Those who have failed to realize this till date must start thinking about global procurement before the competition engulfs them. This could increase the pressure on price competition with corresponding negative consequences on the turnover and profit. However, there is still the opportunity to lead the way and differentiate oneself from the competition.

In most cases the widespread fear of working with foreign suppliers who do not speak any European languages is justified. This also applies to the identification of potential suppliers. Such activities can be successfully executed with the help of an effective plan. In fact, just-in-time delivery is also possible, regardless of how many thousands of kilometers away the supplier is from the buyer.

Fig. 1 Opportunities in global sourcing
Source: Kerkhoff Consulting

What opportunities and challenges does global sourcing offer?

There are many reasons why pragmatic procurement practices ensure profit potential and competitiveness in a sustainable manner. Figure 1 shows the factors on which the success of global sourcing is based, depending on the individual objectives of the company and the situation in the respective countries.

1. Reduction in costs

The most important reason for global sourcing is, without doubt, the potential for reducing material costs and overheads. The enormous success in cost-cutting is reflected in increased profitability within a short span of time. Through Global Sourcing, Chief Executives of Internationally oriented companies can reduce their procurement costs – without losing out on quality. In fact, the transportation costs are already deducted from these values. Low labor and ancillary labor costs, along with generally favorable raw material prices, and the resulting possibility of procuring low-priced preliminary products and services are the essential factors that make worldwide procurement so efficient. These parameters further influence the cost structure of a company in a sustained positive manner. Often, cost-intensive legal conditions or long legal procedures in Western countries can be bypassed through global sourcing. Companies that consistently concentrate on their core competencies and procure uncritical products and services externally and globally will lead the competition in the long term.

In the recent past, competition has also arisen between typical global sourcing countries like China and India. In this regard, the Chinese government has recently announced that it would like to gain a similar strong presence like India in the area of Business Process Outsourcing (BPO). Special economic zones are being developed in this regard. A price competition in BPO is predicted. Furthermore, their government is promoting regions in a targeted manner. Companies that set up base in these regions get subsidies or enjoy massive tax benefits. No wonder these developments have a temporary positive impact on the product pricing. Therefore, companies should focus on procuring from these regions.

2. Improving the negotiating position with existing suppliers

Those suppliers who believe they are in an unchallenged position will be largely inflexible when it comes to negotiating the prices and conditions. Knowledge of international competitors who offer comparable quality at more attractive prices almost »automatically« creates the readiness to make concessions. During discussions, merely mentioning an offer from outside the country sets the stage for orienting the prices to the international markets. At this point, however, it is warned against using the sweeping argument that global sourcing and concretely meeting the requirements is also possible in Asia. The purchasing manager should be very well informed and should be able to clearly demonstrate to the supplier that the requirement can also be met internationally. Otherwise the argument quickly loses its convincing power. Finally, as a rule, the supplier also knows his own competitive situation very well. In this regard, it helps to know where the existing supplier maintains his production locations and from where he procures his preliminary products, because very often the suppliers are also globally active. They either procure globally themselves or already have low-cost production locations abroad.

3. Increasing the supply guarantee

The production of wage-intensive goods is increasingly being relocated from Western countries to low-wage countries. Therefore, global procurement is the only way to create long-term access to products that are no longer manufactured in the local market due to cost reasons. Since decades, we have been aware of this raw materials situation in the market. The disproportionate requirement of rapidly growing countries like China and India for the most varied raw materials just goes to show how quickly the incorrect estimation of supply guarantee of material groups can lead to higher procurement costs. Who would have imagined five years ago the steep rise in steel prices? In the future it could correspondingly come to completely new shortages in entirely different material groups and requirements. An early presence in the important sourcing markets and the knowledge of regional suppliers can help avoid strategic supply shortages combined with massive increases in price. Another example for increasing the supply guarantee is breaking open the monopolistic procurement situations in the domestic markets. A monopolistic or oligopolistic sourcing market brings with it fundamental dependencies and with that, a latent risk of non-supply. Often, we hear from our clients that we should not analyze some material groups at all. In such material groups there are only very few suppliers who have made »agreements like a cartel«. Global sourcing can help break such monopolies. It is only a question of the correct sourcing market research. This is how companies become more flexible, reduce their dependencies and increase their supply guarantee.

4. Optimizing the quality

The access to an increased number of qualified suppliers makes it possible to select from a clearly broad spectrum of offers, often with considerable quality differences. What does this mean? Here are three explanations for the same:

First of all, the common argument that Eastern Europeans and Asians can only supply »cheap goods« is baseless. These countries run a development process in the most diverse regions. 30 years ago, no one would have thought Japan produces high quality automobiles at affordable prices. In the 1990s, one could again see this process happening to Korean companies. Ten years ago, it would have been difficult to imagine that Samsung would manufacture cellular phones and laptops, or Daewoo or Hyundai would manufacture affordable automobiles. The situation of products and services from the »newer« sourcing markets will also develop similarly. Not only Eastern European countries like Hungary, Poland and Turkey, but also countries like India and China have a huge talent pool with the willingness to experiment and learn. There is no reason to talk ill of the quality of products from these countries in the long term as we can keep a tab on quality at the supplier's factory by additional quality checks. Adidas or Puma do this very professionally. As already mentioned, they manufacture almost 100 % internationally. This helps both companies, as long as they conduct strict quality control.

The early identification of key technologies for one's own company is a second important argument for procuring globally and ensuring quality. Those who procure globally profit from these innovative technologies and recognize new trends quite early. Thus, global sourcing can use available experiences of individual sourcing markets in specific sectors in a focused manner. For instance, the Indians are considered the world's best software developers, and other Asian countries for their electronics industry. The cooperation with foreign suppliers can create higher independence from the already existing supplier pool. On the other hand, with its presence in the worldwide sourcing markets, the company can react faster to new trends – an important criterion in times of ever-decreasing product life cycles.

A third argument is that the increasing level of quality offered by international suppliers is a clear stimulus to get themselves moving, both in terms of price and quality.

5. Increased distribution of risk

Internationally, sourcing companies are no longer dependent on the developments in regional sourcing markets. Nationally influencing factors like strikes and supply shortages can be counterbalanced. Ford's painful experiences with its supplier Kiekert could thus have been avoided. Some years ago, the automobile manufacturer procured its door locks exclusively from the German-based supplier and had to stop production of its model series Fiesta and Puma for a few days on account of supply difficulties of the only supplier. Today Ford orders its door locks from several companies; supply problems are now a thing of the past. This makes it clear how cooperating with suppliers from various countries clearly reduces the risk potential. Often in this regard, high political uncertainty is cited as a reason not to procure from certain countries, or in fact to establish production facilities there. This is also correct while making a first superficial observation. To exclude the entire country, however, would be wrong. Here also, it is essential to have a well distinguished selection of the right sourcing markets or the right mix of countries and the suppliers situated there. This is how political unrest, strikes, or natural catastrophes can be bypassed by temporarily relocating the orders to tried and tested suppliers in other countries. In the 1990s the Munich-based fashion house Bogner had to learn this the hard way. Many suppliers were then located in the erstwhile Yugoslavia. When war broke out, Bogner had to relocate its entire collection to other countries in the shortest possible time. If the company had had a healthy mix of several supplier regions, this problem could have been smartly avoided.

6. Opening new sales markets

Those who wish to expand their procurement activities to foreign markets should intensively work to inform themselves about the economic and socio-cultural situation in the respective countries. In the context of these activities, requirements and also sales potential in the regions can be identified without any great additional expense. Close contact with the suppliers and authorities can contribute to significantly improving the success chances of one's own goods when entering a hitherto unopened market. If one wants to sell products in a country that allows imports only in return for being able to supply goods manufactured in that country, then global sourcing can act as an »entry ticket« to the new sales market. This applies just as much if so-called local parts are required. The regulation that a foreign product has to contain a certain percentage of individual parts that are procured from local suppliers, is true in many Asian countries.

7. Efficient reaction to product piracy

In China it is not considered a crime to imitate successful foreign products up to the last detail and then to sell them at cheap prices in the market. The concerned companies can often be spared the effort of engaging a lawyer. They have no chances of compensation for damages unless the global sourcing process has a correct legal backing right from the very beginning. By conducting global sourcing in the Chinese market, however, at least a part of the foregone profits can be compensated for by focused reduction in procurement costs.

8. Anti-cyclical procurement

Strategic, global procurement management identifies and considers economic recessions. If the countries are on an economic downswing or if they have already hit rock bottom, then as a rule this leads to under-utilized production capacities. Often the compulsion to use these to their full capacity brings about a downward price spiral. Attempts are also made to remove high stock inventories at a disproportionate pace. Here one can calculate on favorable procurement costs for preliminary products. The crisis in Asia towards the end of the 1990s to early 2000 was a good example. Seller's markets developed into buyer's markets; all price levels were brought down as a correctional measure. Similar developments were observed during the Internet bust in 2001. Here also, intelligent and strategically functioning purchase managers could register more than proportional price concessions for products and services of all kinds and procure at more favorable prices.

The aforementioned opportunities are very convincing. Global sourcing is, no doubt, also riddled with various challenges that companies should orient themselves to and learn to manage:

a. Delivery time

Those who wish to source globally have to put an end to a dearly held habit. Simply grabbing the telephone receiver and calling for materials at short notice of a few days, or maybe even a few hours, is no longer enough. The delivery time is clearly increasing, unless of course the inventory is clearly expanded – with the accompanying negative effects for the capital lockup. The entire logistics has to be organized professionally in a corresponding manner. Often we hear that it does not make any sense shipping products over such large distances. First, the just-in-time approach is not guaranteed; second, the transportation costs would exceed any actual cost advantages. Just-in-time, however, is possible even in global procurement. With regard to transportation costs, one should also bear in mind that it is more cost-intensive to drive a vehicle carrying raw materials (for example, malt for the brewery industry) from one city to another within the country than to have the goods shipped in from outside the country. This book also touches upon this aspect at a later stage.

b. Difficulties in communication

A language problem leads to serious communication deficiencies. Without a doubt, English is spoken in most sourcing countries. The level of language spoken, however, varies greatly. In Shanghai or Beijing, for example, one would have fewer communication problems, but in more far-flung regions of China, this may not be the case. The situation is similar in the other sourcing countries too. However, one observes time and again that many foreign suppliers speak perfect English, but it is the Western buyers who do not have a satisfactory knowledge of the language. This holds true particularly for buyers from small and medium-sized businesses. It is no surprise, then, that often the very first talks do not meet with any success. Further communication problems arise in the negotiation phase. Here, it is important to consider different country-specific mindsets and strategies. If punctuality and exactness of the agreement, for example, are supreme commandments for the Western businessmen, foreign business partners are often much more unconventional in these areas. If two parties do decide to work together, the deficient communication structure in some countries could make the cooperation difficult. For example, e-mail and the possibility of remote data transmission are not part of the basic set-up in every business.

c. Elaborate market screening

To be able to look »behind the scenes« of a potential supplier from abroad is essentially more difficult than selecting the suppliers from known regions. Often apart from the necessary expense, it is difficult for newcomers without any external help to get reliable information on the future perspective of a potential supplier and his sector. It is of little help to negotiate a seemingly optimal price that in a few weeks shoots up due to massively rising raw material prices. Therefore, a comprehensive, detailed international sourcing market research should be an integral part of every global sourcing attempt. Often, this systematic screening of sourcing markets is not carried out even in the local market. Thus an intensive market research is even more important when considering international markets.

d. Security

The supply uncertainty increases in direct proportion to the geographical distance from the supplier. Besides longer transport distances, political instability, natural catastrophes, or climate risks can influence the security of the delivery of goods. The consistence of the quality is also at risk. There could be a multitude of causes for quality problems. Hence, potential risks during global sourcing should be recognized well in time, so that timely measures can be taken to minimize them. Quality risks can principally be minimized by introducing permanent quality controls, setting up intermediate stores, or by distributing the concrete requirement over several suppliers operating in different regions. A further factor of uncertainty lies in the possible loss of technology. This can refer to patents, drawings, other formal know-how or methodological skills. A professionally conducted global sourcing offers approaches to minimize these risks in the area of technology.

e. Different legal regulations

Until now, the boundaries have been erased only within the EU. When trading with other countries, one has to pay attention to the highly varying custom duty formalities and export regulations. Likewise, the views on the legal consequences of a sales contract are different. Every purchasing manager is therefore advised to get proper legal consultation. The legal practices and the legal systems are very different. The chapter »Legal Aspects of Global Sourcing« looks at this topic more closely.

f. Currency risks

Without a doubt, the management of potential currency risks is often a new challenge of global sourcing, which companies have to learn to handle. Nevertheless, we have seen that in this regard, most companies already have a lot of expertise in the sales and finance departments. The purchase manager seldom makes use of this knowledge. Currency risks have to be calculated, because changing exchange rates can definitely have a negative impact. If the exchange rate of the sourcing country increases and if the sales contract is concluded in the currency of the sourcing country, then the price of the material group to be procured also increases. Today it is recommended to install a professional exchange hedging system to protect oneself from imminent exchange-rate risks.

Important to know:
A regular and consistent analysis of the global sourcing markets brings one to the same conclusion. There is no high-value product that will lose out on quality or image if parts towards its production are procured from abroad. Naturally, the design and technology has to clearly bear the signature of the manufacturer. Many other aspects can, however, be manufactured in or procured from abroad, resulting in cost savings while maintaining the quality standards. It is not surprising that companies are faced with new challenges during global sourcing. What is of more importance is the fact that these challenges can be controlled. There are enough measures in the global sourcing process that can address the arguments made by the critics of international procurement at any time. Naturally, after the implementation until now, the following questions can be raised: »How high should the proportion of foreign components be?«, »Which products can actually be procured internationally?«, and »Which products or services should I rather procure regionally?« There are no straightforward answers to these questions. Material groups in companies always have to be considered individually. These material groups, in turn, consist of individual products. Globally procurable products and services can be ascertained with the help of a material group analysis and value analysis, which are described in chapter four. These analyses give information about

which costs of a product or a process do not make an impact on the quality, consumption, lifecycle or selling price. Everything you manufacture or offer as a service has an individual level of sensitivity. Up to this threshold, parts from low-wage countries can be integrated without any problems, with the precondition that they fulfill your qualitative requirements.

What differentiates global sourcing from other sourcing strategies?

In practice, many different sourcing methods are used. Which strategy is employed would depend on the respective requirements of the company and the complexity of the products to be procured. The »silver bullet« to efficient procurement, in most cases, consists in the target-oriented mix of various methods.

Sourcing strategies can, fundamentally be classified into four categories:
(1) Process-related sourcing strategy
(2) Supplier-related sourcing strategy
(3) Component-related sourcing strategy
(4) Region-related sourcing strategy

Often, in practice, the fourth sourcing strategy, the so-called region-related sourcing strategy, is classified independently. Global sourcing is then subsumed under this category. In many cases, however, the region-specific decision is an integral element of the first three strategies mentioned.

1. Process-related sourcing strategy

The process-related sourcing strategy distinguishes between operational sourcing and advanced sourcing. Operational sourcing is nothing but the normal everyday supplier management. In advanced sourcing, the supplier is involved in the product life cycle of a product of a company making an inquiry right from the very beginning i. e. the research and development conducted by the buyer. The objective is to develop a new product, taking into consideration the cost structure of the product components supplied by the supplier. In this context, often one also speaks of total cost of ownership or of product life-cycle costing. Finally, an attempt is made to outline all receipts and payments from the phase of product development up to the withdrawal of the product from the market. Here, supplier costs require special consideration; they are negotiated for the entire cycle, including price alignments. Global sourcing plays a role particularly in the operational, everyday supplier management. Naturally, advanced sourcing can be carried out globally. The need for coordination, however, is much higher than in simple supplier management. If, instead, advanced sourcing is implemented, there is nothing that speaks against the global request for proposal for components for the entire lifecycle of a product.

2. Supplier-related sourcing strategy

Supplier-related sourcing strategies differentiate between single, dual, and multiple sourcing approaches. Finally, the only question to be answered is how many suppliers should the buyer source one product from. The scope of global sourcing usually includes the so-called multiple approach. This means that the buyer selects several suppliers all catering to the same product, which enables him to spread the volume over many suppliers. In this way the buyer is not dependent on any particular supplier and can also avoid any problems specific to one region. The supply risk remains minimal.

3. Component-related sourcing strategy

Component sourcing, procurement of modules/components, or sourcing of entire systems forms the basis for decisions of a component-related sourcing strategy. Ultimately, the complexity of products is described according to the classic ABC analysis. Often in global sourcing particularly simple process-intensive components with high personnel costs and low supply risks are procured internationally. Nevertheless, one can risk a forecast that we will increasingly be buying complete systems from China or other international sourcing markets in the next three to five years. Many markets are developing at such a rapid pace that in the future we should be prepared to face new competition, even with regard to the more complex systems. In fact, this trend is already making its presence felt in the service sector in the form of BPOs. After all, it is about a system proposition that allows, for example, the selective shifting of commercial functions to India.

The detailing of the sourcing strategies show that differentiating solely on the basis of the region can no longer be regarded as a separate strategy. Rather, such a differentiation forms one aspect in deciding which components, individually or related to a process, need to be procured in what proportion and from how many suppliers, and what sort of supply risk exists for certain products. However, the question is, which products are to be sourced globally, and which products must or should be procured regionally (domestic sourcing)?

Global sourcing is indeed the direct road to achieving enormous cost-cutting potential for many products and in the area of BPO. Everything, however, cannot be procured from abroad if particular supply risks are to be considered. We shall turn to the classic ABC analysis in order to ascertain the most efficient sourcing strategy. To simplify matters, A is used to represent goods with high value that are mostly manufactured as unique pieces. B stands for goods of medium value that are manufactured in medium quantities. C represents goods of low value manufactured in large quantities. While A-parts and certain B-parts are subject to some supply risk because of their respective complexities, the low complexity and lower supply risk of the remaining B-parts and the C-parts create the necessary prerequisites for global sourcing. Figure 2 illustrates the classification of the sourcing strategies.

The matrix also illustrates that a flat classification is indeed possible. There can also be more complex B-parts whose low supply risk allows global sourcing. Finally, the entire material group management of a company should be analyzed on the basis of product complexity and supply risk before a final decision for or against strategic

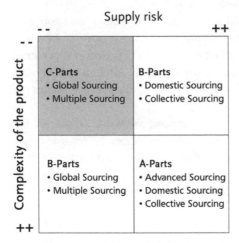

Fig. 2 Sourcing strategies
Source: Kerkhoff Consulting

global procurement can be reached. We present here what an ideal typical process fundamentally looks like.

What does a global sourcing process look like?

Global sourcing makes cross-border procurement an important element of the corporate strategy. Opening up the world's most attractive sourcing markets consists of three phases. The process begins with a comprehensive data analysis (product value and material group analysis). This analysis ascertains which products and materials can be considered for global sourcing. During the second phase (i.e. implementation), suitable markets and potential suppliers are identified and the necessary prerequisites are met in order to integrate the international supplier pool in the present sourcing activities. Procurement controlling, the third phase, aims at ensuring the predetermined quality and reliable supply in the long term.

Global sourcing process

Phase I: Analysis	Phase II: Implementation	Phase III: Controlling
• Product value analysis • Material group analysis	• Requirement/product specification • Market screening • International request for proposal • Supplier assessment and selection • Supply and logistics concept • Supplier negotiations • Award of contract	• Procurement controlling: - Quality - Logistics - Costs - Suppliers - Markets

»Which product components/parts and material groups can be sourced globally?«

»Which supplier can be considered for the delivery?«

»How are quality, logistics, costs, etc. ensured in a sustainable manner?«

Fig. 3 Global sourcing process
Source: Kerkhoff Consulting

1. Data analysis (product value and material group analysis)

The data analysis (product value and material group analysis) is all about analyzing which products or services can be procured from abroad. The criteria for assessment are the relation between weight and value of the product, the required quantities and the possibility of planning it, production requirements, required certificates, duty rates, and logistical requirements. The material group analysis fundamentally accompanies the product value analysis. The method aims at reducing the costs of the products and of their elements for predetermined functions and characteristics. One breaks a product down into its components; strategically important components are separated from strategically unimportant components. The latter (material group analysis) is recommended for a global sourcing approach. On the basis of the data analysis, a first product-related country analysis is carried out. Products are quasi-compared with country competencies. The result helps in deducing a first recommendation of the countries in which a comprehensive market screening should take place.

2. Implementation phase

The implementation phase of professional global sourcing consists of various individual steps that we now present in a first overview:

- *Product specification:* The success of global procurement depends to a large extent on the quality and completeness of the product specifications. The employees responsible in the areas of quality and production should therefore definitely be included in the formulation of the necessary requirements.
- *Market screening:* In market screening, the global sourcing markets that were identified in the analysis phase are checked for qualified, efficient suppliers. This preliminary check is best realized with the help of specific assessment and reference sheets. Market screening, however, is not just based on a comprehensive sourcing market research that takes primary and secondary sources into consideration. It also integrates the specifications laid down during the product analysis.
- *International request for proposal:* A first international request for proposal on the basis of supplier information leads to a first selection of potential suppliers to be considered (long list). From the long list, one can determine which companies can be integrated in the sampling process.
- *Supplier assessment:* The results of the sampling further reduce the circle of potential suppliers (short list). Besides the sampling, the suppliers who are on the short list are assessed on the basis of a comprehensive checklist. The return of the checklist and its evaluation lead to a shorter list. Now, there are only a few suppliers left in the running, and these will be put to the acid test in the form of personal visits to their offices and production facilities. With the help of quality audits, for example, all production facilities that seem suitable for production of the respective requirement are checked in great detail. If the supplier cannot present any current, recognized certifications, then internationally active quality assurance experts need to be assigned the task of testing the manufactured parts. Additionally, the supply and logistics capacities are checked. The effi-

ciency of every international procurement project is measured on the smooth delivery of goods, which is, above all, on schedule. A supply concept should therefore guarantee supply and take the incidental capital lockup costs into consideration. With regard to logistics, companies should work together exclusively with other companies that have the necessary know-how and that have proven their service capability several times. The competence of the logistics experts is, as a rule, documented by a so-called A-license. This license alone is an indicator of the assessment of logistics service providers. The B- and other licenses are not enough.

- *Supplier negotiations:* Due to the completely different mentalities such talks are subject to very special influences that can considerably affect the result. It is not just about prices and conditions in these negotiations, but also about ensuring material quality, as well as measures for guaranteeing supply.
- *Award of contract:* At the end of the negotiations, the decision for or against a cooperation with the selected suppliers has to be carefully prepared. A part of this step is the comparison of the advantages and disadvantages of the respective sourcing markets, the supplier assessments, and the results of the talks with the companies. Likewise, visits to some of the production facilities that are under consideration allow valuable inferences as to whether the cooperation can lead to the desired success. Accordingly, the results are also considered when awarding the final contract. This is finally followed by the operational process of the delivery of goods, including the already mentioned logistics and quality requirements.

3. Procurement controlling

Ensuring the predetermined quality and the timely supply of goods are the central building blocks for the success of your global sourcing strategy. Companies should therefore regularly put their foreign suppliers to the test, just as they do the local suppliers. Therefore, a one-time market screening in the second phase is not enough. Regular checks and possibly new negotiations are a must to ensure the competitive advantages, which have been achieved, in the long term.

The implementation of global sourcing in companies is not merely time-consuming but due to the complexities of international procurement it also demands the exact knowledge of the respective sourcing markets and the specific practices in dealing with international suppliers. Some consulting firms possess this know-how and provide the global sourcing process with theoretical and practical support. They create additional transparency in the international sourcing markets with up-to-date studies on the sector, market, and competition.

How do successful companies profit from global sourcing? Four case studies

In these days of ever-intensifying competition, cross-border procurement is almost becoming a must. Extremely high labor and ancillary labor costs for products and services manufactured in Western countries are forcing companies to source in countries with clearly more attractive general conditions. An exaggerated local patriotism is not advantageous; often, it may in fact lead to a financial disaster. The four companies that are presented on the following pages have long since grasped this: all of them procure globally. All of them register very good sales figures and profits through this future-oriented approach, while their competitors are often struggling to survive.

A medium-sized company relocates its entire production

The situation:
The financial statement of Axel Bree is enough to make the heads of most medium-sized companies jealous. The CEO of this company, which manufactures leather goods near Hanover, announced in the leading German magazine *Manager Magazin*: »We are realizing a fair amount of profit and have as good as no debts.« In 2004, the turnover rose by 7% to almost 50 million euros. Meanwhile,

Bree products are available in more than 80 shops all over the world – from Zurich, Switzerland and Luxembourg to the US, Japan, China, or Korea. The sales network is constantly growing. An extraordinary success in a sector that is currently making the headlines for reasons like clear slump in sales, rising insolvency rates, and layoffs rather than for realizing sparkling profits.

The success strategy:

As the founder of the company, Wolf Peter Bree, suddenly passed away in March 1996, an interim manager first took over as head of the company. A difficult task, because the former company chief was the only one who had all the necessary know-how and the business relations to successfully steer the business into profitable avenues and ventures. In this period, the company suffered a lot of setbacks. This led the management, which included the founder's sons Axel and Philipp Bree since 2001, to bring about a fundamental new orientation. An essential element of the restructuring was relocating the entire production to suppliers. The production facilities at the headquarters in Germany were shut down.

Today Bree does partly manufacture in the former East German state of Thuringia. Most of the products, however, are manufactured in low-cost countries abroad. Suppliers from Italy, Spain, the Czech Republic, Poland, Korea, China, Taiwan, or Vietnam have now taken the place of the German employees. When awarding international contracts, the Brees follow a very clear concept: simple products that are not subject to any fashion trends are manufactured in the Far East. Among these are, for example, nylon bags. Earlier, these timeless articles were manufactured in the Czech Republic. Today, Chinese suppliers have taken over the production, due to the essentially lower labor costs in China. High-value, fashionable ladies' handbags, however, are manufactured in Thuringia, and this does not happen just on account of the short distance. The geographical closeness to the supplier makes it possible to carry out changes in the collection at short notice.

»The tectonics of the international distribution of work never comes to rest,« comments the *Manager Magazin*. After all, the moment Axel Bree discovers any of his competitors' products somewhere that might promise interesting opportunities for his company's turnover and profit, he first identifies the country of its origin. He then sets out to trace potential suppliers in this region via the Internet.

Every year, several hundred new models of bags, travel bags, and small leather goods reach the shelves of the Bree shops. They represent a wide variety of designs that would not have been possible if they were manufacturing all the goods themselves. Consistent globalization is in fact creating new jobs at the company headquarters. When Wolf Peter Bree started production in Isernhagen, the company had 75 employees. Since then, the number has grown to 130. The employees are almost exclusively engaged in designing new products, providing optimal customer service, and further polishing the image of the brand. Sales are also carried out through partners. In Germany Bree has opted for franchising. In the international markets, the importers undertake market development. The company's share in the global market has been continuously increasing in the last few years. The Brees are optimistic that this positive development will continue. A new guideline underlines the strong self-confidence of the family-run company: »Bree – The brand for life, always an idea ahead of the rest.«

French retailer is renowned for tailoring its format and offerings to local tastes

The situation:

If there's any foreign retailer that can hold a candle to Wal-Mart Stores Inc., it's Carrefour. With 86.5 billion US dollars a year in revenues, the Paris company ranks No. 2 worldwide behind the US giant. In the early 1960s, while Wal-Mart founder Sam Walton was still laboring in obscurity in Bentonville, Arkansas, Carrefour was opening the world's first hypermarkets, cavernous retail temples selling everything from lettuce to lawn mowers. Since then it has used fat profits from its French hypermarkets to build the globe's most far-flung retail empire, encompassing more than 10,400 stores in 29 countries. Wal-Mart, by contrast, operates in only 10 countries.

The success strategy:

Its strategy consists of building group market share in each country in which it does business by expanding the type of retailing best suited to the local market and by taking advantage of the way their formats complement one another. Regardless of the business or country in which they work, Carrefour employees share one major focus: the customer. Their personnel aim to satisfy each and every customer expectation with professionalism and to offer the best possible prices for high-quality products and services.

Carrefour's big market share can also be attributed to its flexible marketing strategy and its clear understanding of China's economic policies. Carrefour's flexibility was reflected in its decision to shift its global sourcing base from Southeast Asia and India to China.

In 2001, Carrefour spent 3.5 billion US dollars on purchasing in Asia, of which 61% was purchased in China. Voynet explained that most Chinese goods were low-priced and high quality, which was the main reason the company shifted its global sourcing base to China.

The purchase of goods from China also helped Carrefour to win favor and supportive policies from local governments; since China launched its reform and opening-up policies in the late 1970s, exports had become an important indicator of local government performance. Carrefour's remarkable purchase volume would generate a large export profit margin for local governments. In return, local governments allowed Carrefour to enjoy favorable policies, according to Voynet.

Carrefour is active in all types of retail distribution, primarily food retailing. The Carrefour hypermarkets offer a wide range of food and non-food products at very attractive prices; their shelves stock an average of 80,000 items. Floor areas of hypermarkets range from 5,000 m² to over 20,000 m², and their catchment areas are very large. The supermarkets offer a wide selection of mostly food products, at very competitive prices, in outlets featuring floor areas of 1,000 to 2,000 m². Hard discounters stock around 800 food products, at unbeatable prices, in small stores (from 200 to 800 m²). Half of the products are sold under the Dia brand name. Convenience stores, district shops, offer a range of products covering all food requirements. In addition, they generally offer a range of services.

Electronic commerce is a cyber-market where shopping can be ordered on the Internet and delivered to the door.

A chain of fashion stores expands and raises the turnover by over 10 %

The situation:
At the very first instance, the business idea of H&M hardly sounds original. »Fashion and quality at the best price« is what the Swedish company wants to provide in its close to 1,100 stores in more than 20 countries. Other boutique chains also draw in customers with similar declarations and, in the end offer the customers nothing more than average goods at not particularly attractive prices. Things are, however, different in the company founded by Erling Persson in 1947. H&M actually offers trendy fashion and classics at absolutely affordable prices. Word has long since spread among the customers, and this has paved the way for continuous profitable growth in a sector that has been complaining about falling sales and threateningly rising insolvency rates since many years.

The success strategy:
The company's own design department develops the collections, in order to constantly be able to offer the latest fashion. H&M does not manufacture its own collections; instead, the concern has more than 20 production offices all over the globe – ten each in Europe and Asia, and one each in Africa and Central America. The approximately 700 employees of these offices are, to a large extent, recruited from around that region, and they maintain contact with the 700 or so suppliers. Their task is placing the order with the right supplier, monitoring the quality, and taking care to see that the working conditions for the employees of the supplier are favorable.

There are many factors that determine the country from where a product is ordered. Besides the price, the other factors are delivery times, import regulations, and quality requirements. This decision process has led to H&M ordering some 50% of its goods from

Europe and the rest mainly from Asia. At present, the delivery times are anywhere between two weeks and six months. In the last three years, the company succeeded in reducing this time frame by 15 % to 20 % and, in this way, in further increasing the flexibility. Detailed planning and optimal order deadlines are the essential reasons for this improvement. A short delivery time is not always particularly advantageous. Articles that are ordered in large quantities, such as basic designs and children's clothes, are ordered several months before the desired delivery deadline. Trendy designs, on the other hand, have to reach the stores in a very short time, because these are »in« only for a limited time.

The close cooperation between the production offices and the suppliers makes it possible to order the necessary material well in time. The manufacture and testing of prototypes is likewise carried out in the international production offices – one more prerequisite for increasingly shorter delivery times. A continuous process of improvement aims at further reducing the time frame between the order and the delivery. »Because,« according to H&M, »the later an order can be placed, the lesser is the risk of buying the wrong thing and the higher is the flexibility of the stores in replenishing their stock during the season with successful products.«

A polished distribution system makes it possible to transport the goods from a foreign supplier to the respective store anywhere in the world on schedule. Every link in the closely connected logistics chain is controlled by H&M. The company can monitor all activities at any time, and it also undertakes the roles of importer, wholesaler, and retailer. Additionally, the consistent improvement in IT has contributed in reducing the delivery times and optimizing supply to the chain of stores.

The success of this exemplary procurement strategy has led to a continuous rise in the profits of the Swedish concern. The discontinuation of trade quotas for Asian textiles since early 2005 has left the sources of profits in a particularly effervescent state. If this easing of the quotas and the lower purchase price that comes with it continue to exist even in the future, H&M expects even more pronounced jumps in its profits. Further expansion is a matter already agreed upon since a long time. The brand is increasingly achieving the status of a cult product.

A Spaniard makes global sourcing a building block for the success of Germany's largest automobile manufacturer

The situation:

When Dr. José Ignacio López de Arriortúa took charge of the purchasing department of Volkswagen in 1993, an appalled groan was let out by the line of suppliers of the concern based in Wolfsburg, Germany. Even during his term as head of purchasing of General Motors Europe, the Spaniard had grown to become the most feared opponent of the suppliers. He did not leave it at just making it very clear to the suppliers, with two fisted words, that they had not for a long time considered all cost-cutting potential with their calculations. López performed convincing work of a completely unknown kind: during his rounds through the production facilities of his domestic and foreign suppliers, he discovered in the shortest time, a plethora of possibilities for improvement. »Inaki«, as his fans call him, immediately corrected some defects himself by simply taking off his sports coat and lending some workstations new efficiency with a couple of manual tasks.

The success strategy:

In the Volkswagen concern, global sourcing was a procurement tool even before López made his entry. For »Inaki,« however, the activities connected with it were far from enough. He set out with his team to structure the global procurement and thus to give it a much greater efficiency.

Two process departments were established then – one for the area of global sourcing and the other for advanced sourcing, known as forward sourcing at Volkswagen. The latter refers to finding and cooperating with suppliers who are then included from the stage of development of a new automobile model. Subsequently, they supply the respective part during the complete product life cycle at a price predetermined by the buyer. With the introduction of forward sourcing, López set a milestone in the automobile industry. Billions were saved in the automotive sector.

The illustrated goal of global and forward sourcing was the optimization of customer benefit through global procurement marketing. Therefore, the Corporate Sourcing Committee, a globally positioned organization with its head office at the company headquarters in Wolfsburg, was established. So-called Local Purchasing Teams at the international production locations of the entire Volkswagen concern, as well as in important cities like Tokyo, Sydney, Brussels, Shanghai, Moscow, and Mexico, were assigned the task of searching for potential suppliers in their region for every order with a volume upwards of then 157,000 US dollars. A decisive advantage for Volkswagen and other brands of the company: all potential suppliers around the globe were considered. The danger that a »good friend« of the buyer would bag the order without a request for proposal was averted.

The Corporate Sourcing Committee met once a week. These meetings were not just attended by the brand purchasing managers and representatives of the Local Purchasing Teams. The areas of development, logistics, and finance were just as much a part of the round of discussions. Last but not the least, the head of purchasing, López, did not miss the opportunity to experience first hand how successfully his team worked. The buyer responsible for every order had to present three charts to this top-class team. The first overview, the »local bidding list«, showed the list of available offers. It was completely clear that each one who received only little response to his inquiry would have to deal with the criticism of his superiors.

The second chart was called »comparison sheet«. Here, all interesting offers were compared to each other – including a long-term consideration and the cost-cutting possibilities additionally offered. The third overview, the »recommendation sheet«, showed the savings potential of individual offers over the entire life cycle of the product. The final decision process began after reviewing the three assessments. »There were quite heated discussions among those involved from the different departments,« recalls Gisbert Langheim. He was then the head of purchasing of the Volkswagen subsidiary Skoda and is today among the consultants of Kerkhoff Consulting. In just three years, the Volkswagen concern saved over 7.5 billion euros with the combination of global and forward sourcing.

When it was about procuring parts or about renegotiating manufactured goods for models the López team helped the suppliers to design their production process more efficiently. By doing so Volkswagen and its suppliers profited equally and the amounts that were saved were shared. Global and forward sourcing à la López led to a massive improvement in profits for all suppliers who were willing to allow themselves to be helped by López or his employees. This is why the number of existing suppliers remained largely unchanged even after Inaki's entry and his clear direction towards global procurement. Gisbert Langheim remarks, »Our first concern was to hold a mirror in front of the existing suppliers and to show them what the international competition can accomplish.«

Although the name López no longer strikes a very positive chord in Volkswagen: Global and forward sourcing continues to be the building blocks for the success of the automobile manufacturers from Wolfsburg and their subsidiaries.

What general conditions are required for efficient global sourcing?

Those who wish to make global procurement the profit driver of their company should not restrict themselves to orienting only the purchasing department to the new type of sourcing. Continuously successful global sourcing is possible only when a host of traditional processes are adapted to it and a new way of thinking enters the company. Many companies have not yet recognized the fact that modern strategic procurement includes national and international suppliers and that it means much more than merely ordering goods at the best possible prices. For this reason, implementing and monitoring a profit-oriented global procurement is to be given top priority. For Mrs. Alicja Wojciechowska, former Head of Purchasing Department of Accor Poland, a worldwide leading metals distributor, this is a very important prerequisite. According to her, »extensive research, several in-depth consultations with suppliers and site visits require considerable resources in terms of time and personnel. This process is only successful when all concerned departments in the company work hand in hand. Hence, professional support from outside is of great use.«

Almost all processes in the company are affected by the new direction towards the international sourcing markets. This means, for example, that available logistical concepts have to be thoroughly revised and have to be designed for the new requirements as a result of the emerging global supplier network. Longer delivery times lead to changes in the order intervals and volumes. The quality control in most cases that could be carried out during receipt of goods with little time and effort is not enough any more. The employees in the area of research and development have to deal with suppliers who might work with different production procedures. The company lawyers need additional knowledge to master international contract law. Language abilities have become more important than they already are. New techniques of communication take the place of the telephone as the main connection between the purchasing department and the suppliers. The necessary changes naturally demand a certain amount of time and money. The cost-cutting potential, however, balances these investments in the middle term, mostly in fact within a few months.

Chapter 3
Global Sourcing – The Most Attractive Regions for International Procurement

Nearly 80% of all business enterprises justify their decision to adopt global sourcing with the aim of permanently reducing their labor costs and ancillary labor costs. This makes it obvious to select the country with the lowest labor costs. Labor costs, however, is just one of the many criteria that must be considered when deciding to procure from or manufacture in a foreign country. It is the aim to look for an optimum combination of necessary costs, largely calculable risks, attainable efficiency, and finally, favorable labor costs. Which country or which region closely meets these requirements would largely depend on the orientation of the company. The company could, for example, be interested in exploring the possibilities of developing the sourcing country as a future market for its goods. And naturally, no company would want to enter a country that is not expected to register any economic growth in the foreseeable future.

Among the most relevant sourcing regions are emerging economies; in other words, countries that are experiencing a relatively successful industrial development. In the global auto industry in the 1990s, the rapid growth in sales and production between 1990 and 1997 came largely from the emerging markets rather than the triad regions (North America, the European Union and Japan). However, for some of these markets the downturn that followed was substantial and prolonged. Rapid technological advancements make fragmenting of activities in all stages of a production value chain increasingly possible. Some segmented activities can be performed in different locations worldwide and reintegrated again into global value chains and global production networks. When sometime in the future these developing countries become industrialized countries with a general framework that equals the impractical situation in Europe, it would be worthwhile to then put them to the test reg-

Global Sourcing. Gerd Kerkhoff
Copyright © 2006 WILEY-VCH Verlag GmbH & Co. KGaA, Weinheim
ISBN: 3-527-50232-7

ularly and to assess whether this sourcing region needs to be changed. With respect to procurement orders for medium- and large-sized companies, consulting firms analyze economic regions all over the world according to their potential yield. The result of this analysis is very clear: China, India, and the countries of Eastern Europe, including Turkey, are literally predestined for global sourcing in the current scenario. This could change in the next few years. But for the moment these countries offer the most attractive cost-cutting potential. It is completely possible that in the near future Brazil shall also join the league of appropriate sourcing countries; though only after the economic and political situation in the country further stabilizes.

The most important criteria when selecting the country

The decision for or against a particular sourcing country is a multi-level process (see figure 4: Country Assessment Portfolio).

The matrix begins with identifying countries that are in a position to fulfill the necessary prerequisites for meeting specific needs in the context of procurement. One of these prerequisites is regional proximity. Buyers who must depend on short delivery times will have to be prepared for comparatively high organizational effort and costs if they wish to source from China or any other Asian country. The supplier making a prompt visit to dispel an existing problem

Fig. 4 Country Assessment Portfolio
Source: Kerkhoff Consulting

»in a jiffy« also does not apply. It is also worth remembering that the further away the sourcing country lies from the company headquarters, the more different are the mentalities and business miens of the partner. With such geographical distances, the factors of particular significance are the level of education and the qualifications of the employees. The aforementioned emerging economies, however, are an exception, at least in their industrial centers. Indian engineers, for example, are easily comparable to their Western counterparts in terms of technical knowledge. Meanwhile, privately run workshops in China fulfill, at the very least, average Western European quality standards and are increasingly gaining experience in exports. Not to mention the high qualifications and enormous commitment of the employees and company heads in the EU accession countries and Turkey.

The level of labor costs is naturally very important, but as mentioned earlier, not the singular deciding criterion. Exception: the manufacture of a product procured internationally that demands an extremely labor-intensive manufacturing process. Along with the labor costs, the national tax rate and the rate of subsidy are equally important cost factors.

A country that passes the first level of the selection procedure also passes through the second. In this second level, the focus is on getting a feel of the current and future political as well as economic situation of the potential sourcing market. There is a list of significant tools that help assess the same. It is thus possible to gauge the index of economic freedom of the concerned country, its creditworthiness, and its estimated economic growth. It is also recommended to factor in corruption in the selection procedure. This factor unfortunately plays an imperative role in economically developed countries just as much as it does in developing countries or emerging economies.

Changes in currency exchange rates could contribute significantly to the economic success or failure of global sourcing in a relatively unknown market. In this context, it is important to know that procurement orders are settled in euros in Eastern Europe, whereas Asian countries prefer the US dollar. Due to currency fluctuations, there is a potential of additional risk for buyers in other currencies. The same problem could be created when the exchange rate of the sourcing country increases, causing the cost for the buyer to surge up as well. Modern exchange hedging systems help in reducing these risks.

A prospective buyer should also analyze the degree of democratic freedom in the sourcing country before he reaches his final decision. It is important to find out whether the citizens enjoy unrestricted civil rights and whether there is a social security system for the employees. Should this not be the case, there is a potential threat of conflicts, which could have a negative impact on the guaranteed supply of goods.

The most significant tools for country assessment

Unfortunately, it is not possible to entirely exclude a certain degree of risk when deciding on a sourcing country. There is a list of recognized ratings that facilitate the broad comparison between potential countries, throw light on many important factors, and thus greatly reduce the risk of arriving at a wrong decision. Some of the ratings are:

- *Business Competitiveness Index (BCI):* The World Economic Forum annually updates the BCI, which assesses the capacity of the organizations of the particular country of surviving in the international competitive environment with their service portfolios. To arrive at a result, the quality of management and the microeconomic fundamentals are assessed. The latest ranking can be found under: www.weforum.org.
- *Growth Competitiveness Index (GCI):* This index is also published annually by the World Economic Forum and reflects the potential for economic growth in a country. The GCI is founded on three factors: the macroeconomic environment, the commitment of the concerned country in promoting the economy, and its technological potential. The latest ranking can be found under: www.weforum.org.
- *Index of Economic Freedom:* The Index of Economic Freedom is based on factors, updated annually, that closely contribute to

the development of competitiveness and social prosperity. Some of these factors are: the framework for foreign investment, monetary policy, taxes, custom duties, government spending ratio, and government intervention in the economy. The lower the government intervention, the better is the development of the Index of Economic Freedom, and with that the economy of the country. The latest ranking can be found under: www.heritage.org/research/features/index.

- *Sovereign risks:* Globally active rating agencies like Standard & Poor's and Moody's assess at regular intervals the likelihood that a country cannot or does not want to fulfill its financial obligations. Political and economic trends, like political stability or instability, changes in the employment market, development of economic growth, national debt, and interest rates, are included in these sovereign risks. A comparison between the ratings of various agencies clearly shows how in some cases the results are significantly different from one another. The latest ranking can be found under: www.standardpoors.com and www.moodys.com.

- *Comparison between industrial labor costs:* The divide between labor costs and ancillary labor costs in each country is enormous. There are unfortunately no regularly updated statistics on the situation existing in all sourcing countries. While comparing costs, companies essentially have to rely on their own research. In doing so, the Chambers of Commerce abroad offer significant help by providing current information. Figure 5 gives an idea of the cost advantages that can arise from global sourcing or production abroad, provided that the aforementioned general conditions are fulfilled.

- *Transparency International Corruption Perceptions Index (CPI):* Transparency International is the only globally active non-governmental organization that has taken it upon itself to exclusively combat corruption at the level of awarding public contracts. The CPI has clearly documented the enormous impact of corruption on the economy of many countries for the year 2004. To do so, the CPI conducted its research in 146 countries, collecting information from parties involved in the areas of economics, trade, and capital goods.

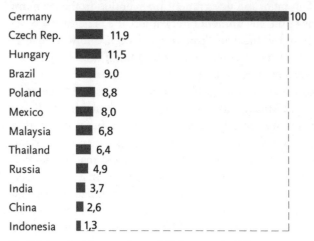

Industrial labor costs per hour, including social security contributions Germany Index = 100		
Germany		100
Czech Rep.		11,9
Hungary		11,5
Brazil		9,0
Poland		8,8
Mexico		8,0
Malaysia		6,8
Thailand		6,4
Russia		4,9
India		3,7
China		2,6
Indonesia		1,3

Fig. 5 Comparison between industrial labor costs in different countries
Source: Kerkhoff Consulting

The alarming result:
106 countries received less than five of a possible ten points. Among these, 60 countries had less than three points; a result that clearly points to the deep-rooted corruption in many countries. The latest ranking can be found under: www.transparency.de.

As we have seen, the final decision on the sourcing country can only be made after considering the whole picture and depends on the individual requirements of the company. If a hasty decision is reached without a careful analysis of the potential sourcing region, one runs the risk of failure. In such cases, the cost-cutting potential, at least in the middle term, remains largely untapped. In addition, the burden of costs for the unsuccessful efforts of trying to establish oneself in a new market weighs heavily on the company's profit and loss statement.

Sourcing market China

Hardly any other country in the world today has undergone such an extent of change in the recent past as China. When the People's Republic was declared in 1949, the countries of the world wondered how the Chinese government would manage to support its huge population. After over 55 years, the population of the country has touched 1.3 billion. The world's most populous country has today become one of the leading exporting nations. Cellular phones and computers have become commonplace, at least in cities, and cars are fast replacing bicycles as the preferred mode of transport. The country's amazing rise began after Mao's death in 1977, after which the centrally administered economy was progressively reformed. The clear direction is towards a market economy. The reforms reached their peak in March 2004, when the constitution laid down the protection of private property. China's entry into the World Trade Organization (WTO) towards the end of 2001 was a clear indication of the country shaking itself out of the isolation of many years and opening itself to the rest of the world. In spite of the recent developments, however, China continues to be one of the poorer emerging economies, with a per capita income of a little over 1,000 US dollars.

Convincing economic figures

With the newfound strength of the Chinese economy, it has grown in significance as a sourcing market, a ready market for goods, and a manufacturing location. Despite some controversial discussions about the duration of this economic boom, many decision makers of the German economy are of the opinion that a commitment in this huge market is almost a must for any farsighted company. Siemens' chairman of the supervisory board, Heinrich von Pierer, is convinced that the risk of not investing in China is much higher than the risk of having a presence in the country. To further support this stand, foreign investments in China rose from 41 billion US dollars in 2000 to 57 billion US dollars in 2003. The country is well under way to becoming the most sought-after production location in the world today.

The continuous growth is also reflected in the constant upward trend of the Gross Domestic Product (GDP). Since 1978 in China, the annual growth rate of the GDP has been an average 8%, while, in comparison, the EU countries had to be satisfied with a meager 0.5% growth in 2003. Based on the GDP, the »red giant« ranks among the ten largest economies worldwide. If the same pace of growth continues, it will overtake France and England by 2007. According to a study of the Economic Intelligence Unit, Germany will have to be prepared to be ousted by China as the third largest economy by 2017 at the latest. If one considers the parity in purchasing, China is already in second place internationally. The same dynamics are evident in the development of industrial value added processes, which increased by about 17% in the years 2003 and 2004. The proportion of profit generated by state-owned undertakings was 46% in 2003. The proportion of privately run businesses is rapidly increasing. Between 2001 and 2002 alone, the number of these businesses rose by close to 36%.

The impressive economic growth has until now been restricted to the eastern parts of the country that lie along the coast. Among the most important industrial sectors are iron and steel, coal, engineering, armament, textiles, production of petroleum and cement, chemical fertilizers, shoes, toys, electronics, and telecommunications. While foreign investors are mostly concentrated in and around Guangdong, Jiangsu, and Shanghai, the regions in the interior of the country still remain largely removed from the benefits of the growing attraction of China. The government, however, is trying to draw interested companies into the central provinces by easing taxes in these regions.

It is very likely that companies looking at establishing themselves in China in the long run will enter into joint ventures with Chinese companies. Such cooperation, however, is not an advantage just for the Chinese business partners. The foreign investors benefit from the market knowledge and existing customer contacts of their partners. In addition, the know-how and experience of the Chinese counterparts increase due to such close cooperation, which has a positive impact on the sustainable profitability of the joint venture.

There is a huge opportunity to profit from the sustained boom in China. Being present in China, however, requires perseverance, underlines Rainer Häupl, the Senior Procurement Commercial Vehicles/Asian Alliances at Daimler Chrysler. He comments, »If I decide for China, then I must live with all that comes with it and learn to successfully deal with it.«

Sino-European economic relations improving constantly

Chinese exports to the EU surged by 38% to 84.8 billion US dollars in the first 10 months of the year 2004, while Chinese imports rose 30% to 57.5 billion US dollars. Economic and trade relations between the EU and China have developed in step with the latter's emergence on the global economic scene.

China overtook Japan in 2002 to become the EU's second-largest trading partner outside Europe, with a trade volume of over 115 billion US dollars. The EU has replaced Japan to become China's largest trading partner after its newest enlargement into a 25-member bloc.

The Chinese Ministry of Commerce estimated that the trade volume between China and European Union is expected to top 200 billion US dollars in 2005. Bilateral trade in the first 11 months of 2005 reached 196.78 billion dollars, about 15.3% of China's total foreign trade, a year-on-year growth of 23.6%, according to statistics from China Customs.

European Union remained China's largest trade partner in 2005 and China was European Union's second largest trade partner. In 2005 China exported more high-tech products to the European market than before, and European Union took the place of the United States to become China's top exporting market for mechanical and electronic products.

Soaring trade also stimulated investment and technology introduction. European Union has been China's largest technology supplier and the fourth largest investor in China. By the end of October 2005, China had introduced 20,925 technologies, with a contracted value amounting to 87.1 billion dollars. At that time, European companies set up 22,076 businesses in China, bringing the contracted investment volume to 84.7 billion dollars, with actual investment hitting 46.7 billion dollars.

The high-tech sector, including the maglev trains, Air Bus planes and nuclear power stations, has been the key fields attracting European investment. While expanding its business in China's rich coastal areas, European companies also cast its eyes on China's western part and the old industrial base in northeast China.

More European companies are moving their plants and research centers to the above areas, which are identified for their abundant labor force. These areas have thus successful realized increased European investment in recent years. A medium- and long-term plan for Sino-European trade is being drafted, and bilateral trade volume is expected to hit 300 billion US dollars in the near future. Steps are being taken to boost trade with European Union countries in the coming years and at the same time to encourage Chinese companies to make investment in Europe.

Opportunities and challenges in conducting business in China

According to forecasts, the economic growth of the last few years will continue, although at a slower rate. Chinese companies, however, are increasingly taking this foreseeable development into consideration with respect to their expansion strategies and are setting their sights on foreign markets. This also creates attractive opportunities for the development of foreign investment. From the point of view of Western companies, the initial phase demands patience and ample investment of time. Especially due to the different mentalities and business miens, one or two years could easily go by until a close partnership being a basis for mutual growth can be formed.

Despite the continual above average growth, the Chinese economy does indeed harbor some risks and threats. Corruption, for example, is commonplace. Costs of raw material, too, are drastically rising and are threatening to wipe out the savings made on labor costs in the long run. Some areas are already facing overcapacity. One must also not underestimate the penchant of the Chinese to copy successful products. It is often possible, though, to successfully counteract this tremendous drive. Thus, many companies assign Chinese suppliers with the task of manufacturing semi-finished goods that do not disclose any method of obtaining the end product.

Procuring tools in China – Interesting alternative not just for the automobile industry

The extraordinary economic growth in China is also impacting the automobile industry. In 2003 alone, over two million automobiles were manufactured. This number is expected to rise to around 3.2 million in 2005. Thanks to increasing purchasing power the sector will grow further, but at the same time it will also have to face very tough competition. Prompted by this development in the past, many automobile manufacturers, such as Volkswagen, BMW, Ford, General Motors, Fiat, Peugeot, and Citroën, to name a few, have set up their own production facilities in China. As is common in this sector, the suppliers are requested to settle down in close proximity to their buyers; some of them, in fact, offer to do so themselves. This is how not just mega-suppliers like Delphi and Bosch have their own production facilities. Larger medium-sized companies, too, like the air-conditioning and cooling systems specialist Behr, have set up their plants in the centers of automobile industry. More suppliers are bound to follow.

Until recently, car makers and their suppliers sourced their material to a large extent – up to the volume that has to be procured in China as per the Local Regulations – in their home countries, and therefore had to bear high transportation costs. The massively rising cost pressure that the manufacturers exert on the suppliers, however, is forcing a re-orientation, because there is hardly any potential to cut costs at home. In China, too, the competition has intensified due to growing overcapacities, and this is forcing manufacturers to reduce prices, which could partially be compensated for by the concessions offered by the suppliers of components. Volkswagen, once an international pioneer in the Chinese automobile market, after having enjoyed many profitable years in this market, will have to incur losses, for the first time, of possibly over 400 million euros in 2005. There is, therefore, the likelihood of further demands on the suppliers. As a result, it has become a must for manufacturers in this sector to have their own production facilities in China, or at least to acquire reliable and reasonably priced suppliers.

The Kerkhoff study »Procuring tools in China – Opportunities for the automobile industry«, therefore made it its aim to analyze whether relocating tool construction to Chinese workshops would be economically efficient today, and whether the quality of the products would then correspond to the high international requirements of the automobile manufacturers. The results of this study can be useful in setting up own procurement activities in China, as well as for analyzing the competition. They are not specific only to the automobile industry but can also be applied to any other industry.

The study was conducted in early 2005 in cooperation with Forum China and the German Chamber of Commerce in Shanghai. The results are based on analysis, surveys, and interviews with almost 30 international automobile companies and over 400 tool manufacturers. The interviews were conducted in Chinese, which allowed additional impressions and insights being incorporated into the assessment. The most important results of the analysis can be summarized as follows:

- The Chinese tool market is rapidly growing. The last ten years have seen the turnover rising from around 1.34 billion US dollars to close to 5.49 billion US dollars. The average annual growth rate between 1993 and 2003 amounted to 15.2%. Experts believe this development will continue.
- Chinese tools are increasingly gaining acceptance abroad. The comparison of import and export volumes underlines the growing reputation of Chinese tools among foreign companies. The amount of tools exported from China in 1994 was worth 39 million US dollars. In a span of ten years, this number increased almost tenfold to an impressive 336 million euros in 2003. Tool imports, meanwhile, almost doubled from 675 million euros to 1.4 billion euros.
- The number of suppliers has also steadily increased. Between 1987 and 2003, the number of companies engaged in tool construction in China rose from 6,000 to 20,000. At the same time, the number of employees in this sector rose from 300,000 to 500,000. Most of the companies established in the last few

years are privately run. A significant advantage for potential clients, because, as against state-run companies, private companies have fewer employees and consequently greater flexibility and readiness in adapting to essential norms and requirements.

- Die-casting tools dominate. The interviewed tool manufacturers produce over 50 % of all die-casting tools. This focus is a result of Chinese industry's long years of experience in the areas of household and electronic consumer durables. These segments principally require tools for die-casting. Casting (21.5 %) and die-cutting tools (19.8 %) occupy the second and third places respectively. An important note: most of the manufacturers concentrate on a particular set of tools. There are indeed some large tool manufacturers, mostly state run, who offer a broader spectrum of products. They can, however, not compete with the privately run companies when it comes to quality.
- The performance spectrum of the automobile industry has been broadened. Due to their extensive know-how, Chinese tool manufacturers produce above all die-casting tools for automobile manufacturers. Most companies, however, are working very keenly on strengthening the die-cutting tools sector.
- There is a tremendous interest in foreign markets. For many private companies, export is increasingly becoming part of the daily business. Many export close to 75 % of their entire production, thus becoming interesting partners for global sourcing in China. State-run companies, on the other hand, produce mainly for the local market.
- 40 % of the interviewed tool manufacturers are exporting since one to three years. One-fourth of the companies are still newcomers and are engaged in export since less than a year. This goes to show that in most cases there is some experience in exports. Setting up business relations requires, nonetheless, a great extent of care and perseverance.
- There is a great readiness to improve quality standards. 90 % of the interviewed tool manufacturers are convinced of the important role of exports in the success of their business, which is why companies are ready, more than ever, to adapt to the

requirements of their foreign clients. Amounting to a mere 4%, the number of companies that do not consider foreign trade to be of importance is miniscule.
- The course has been set for growth. The will to further expand business is very strong among the Chinese tool manufacturers. Almost all companies plan to expand in the next few years and explore new markets. This will further increase the competition within the sector, much to the advantage of the buyers.

The results of the study »Procuring tools in China – Opportunities for the automobile industry«, as well as our experience with the Chinese tool manufacturing industry bring us to the following conclusions:

- Tools in the so-called low-end segment (low complexity), and partially also in the middle-end segment (medium complexity), can be easily procured from China without having to sacrifice on the quality. The high-end segment (high complexity) is being strengthened by leading tool manufacturers in the country.
- Costs can be cut by up to 60% or more in the tool market of the People's Republic.
- The sector is indeed ready to adapt to new clients. However, buyers must be prepared to face some risks and setbacks.
- Most differences are due to problems in communication or quality.

Besides, some automobile manufacturers have already recognized the quality and affordability of Chinese tool manufacturers. They procure up to 80% of all their requirements in China.

Important addresses for those interested in China are:
- German Office for Foreign Trade, www.bfai.com
- German Chamber of Commerce in China, www.ahk.de/eng/index.html
- German Center for Industry and Trade, www.germancentre.org.cn/english/index–engl.htm

Sourcing market India

The reforms introduced in 1991 have seen India on the way to a social market economy. Improved infrastructure and investments in health and education are expected to further support this new direction. Privatization initiatives, though, are again being lightly held in rein.

The growth of the Gross Domestic Product (GDP) underlines the increasing economic strength of the country and its 1.1 billion people. Industry and services have been the sectors that have shown tremendous development. The industrial sector today contributes almost 25% to the GDP, while the proportion of the services sector is more than 50%. According to a forecast of the Asian Development Bank, this trend will continue in the next few years. Although India now ranks among the most innovative and high-performing nations worldwide in the fields of information technology, pharmacy, and biotechnology, it still belongs to the group of developing countries. The country's leading role in the BPO sector will also see tremendous growth in the future, since not only banks and insurance companies but, increasingly, industrial enterprises are also outsourcing their accounts, handling of claims, and in fact even their controlling tasks to India. For a long time now, Indian specialists have been creating labor-intensive construction drawings for a whole list of American, British, German and South-African engineering companies.

Despite the continuing boom, a quarter of the population still lives below the poverty line, with less than 1 US dollar a day at their disposal. 80% of the population must make do with less than 2 US dollars a day. Nevertheless, there is a huge growth in terms of qualification. Every year, about 250,000 well-qualified engineers enter the job market and thus contribute to the innovative power and competitiveness in plant construction and the automobile industry. Meanwhile, there is a steep rise in the number of Indian students at elite international universities, accounting for an increased know-how.

Dynamic development of international trade

Today, the EU is India's most significant trade partner. The EU is India's largest trading partner and main source of foreign inward investment. The EU accounted for 23% of India's exports and imports in 2004. India ranks as EU's 12th trading partner accounting for 1.7% of EU exports and imports. In 2004, EU imports from India amounted to 16,3 billion euros (covering mainly textiles/clothing, agricultural products and chemicals) while EU exports to India amounted to 17 billion euros (covering mostly machinery and chemical products). During 2004 EU-India trade increased by 17% and has increased with an annual average of 6% between 2000 and 2004.

Given its developing country status, India's exports to the European Union benefit from reduced tariffs (under the EU Generalised System of Preferences). Bilateral trade in services has grown substantially in recent years and in 2003 India's exports of services to the EU amounted to 2.8 billion euros, while the EU's services exports to India amounted to 2.6 billion euros.

The easing of investment boundaries is expected to motivate many more foreign companies to make an aggressive entry into the Indian market. Up until now, many investors have held themselves back, owing to insufficient infrastructure, the debilitating bureaucracy, and corruption. Nevertheless, the last few years have seen many joint ventures being set up. The experience of foreign companies has largely been positive. They have been registering over 20% growth annually in turnover and earnings.

Close economic relations with United Kingdom

The United Kingdom is the third largest investor in India. The important factor is that British companies are major players in India's service sector, for example in banking, insurance and education. On the other side, India is a growing economy. There is a mood of optimism and self-confidence in India with its excellent showing on the forex exchange reserves, good harvests, over 8% GDP growth and the stock market at a new high.

Trade relations between the UK and India have never been as good as in the last couple of years. In the first nine months of the year 2003, bilateral trade grew by a fifth, while exports of British goods to India jumped 27%. But these figures do not tell the full story of the economic relationships.

About a quarter of the trade between the UK and India is no longer in goods, but in services. The impressive economic growth registered by India and its potential have in a way made the UK identify it as one of the three key countries (along with the US and China) with whom it needs to work closely in the coming years. The new economy and the knowledge-based industries will be the building blocks for new cooperation in the coming years. Both the countries are working out the necessary details.

India – World's leader in Business Process Outsourcing (BPO)

India has become the frontrunner in the booming BPO sector, thanks to highly qualified people and the country's leading position in information technology and communications. In many Western countries, the term BPO is publicly looked upon with great suspicion. BPO means outsourcing of business processes with a high proportion of IT, and the term »outsourcing« is generally seen as just another term for slashing jobs.

It is, however, becoming increasingly common for Western companies (especially in the US) to award contracts for the computing of wages and salaries, and standardized processes in finance, accounts, and personnel administration to Indian BPO units, which competently perform the tasks from a distance of thousands of kilometers. BPO is much more than just call centers, as is often presumed in Europe.

An increasing number of international banks and insurance companies are discovering this service in order to make optimal use of the untapped profit potential, and the sector has been booming. According to a study of the market research institute IDC, BPO grew globally by 8% in 2003, generating a turnover of 405 billion US dollars. IDC expects this figure to increase further to more than 680 billion US dollars by 2008.

The advantages of the new strategy are obvious:
- The company undertaking outsourcing can concentrate on its core competencies much more than before.
- There is a significant reduction in costs.
- The service provider assures Best Practices and top technology.
- The company strengthens its competitive position through, among others, greater customer satisfaction, higher efficiency, and quicker access to the market.

European banks and insurance companies discover BPO

Most credit institutes, regardless of whether they are highly renowned or medium-sized, are intensively working on reducing their costs. Large banks have been making headlines for reducing their workforce and closing down their branch offices. Smaller institutes, too, have been following in the same footsteps. From the early 1990s to 2004, the number of banks in most countries has almost halved, making it increasingly difficult to close any further branches without irking their clients or driving them to Internet banking. BPO is indeed gaining in importance, although it is aggressively used only by a few. Insurance companies are only just beginning to consider following this trend.

Kerkhoff Consulting analyzed the current situation and interviewed credit institutes and insurance companies about their outsourcing activities and plans. Benchmarking discussions with international banks brought us to the clear conclusion that the term BPO has long since not been enjoying the position it deserves. In this way, an enormous potential for cost-cutting remains untapped.

International credit institutes and insurance companies are the frontrunners in BPO

In international credit institutes and insurance companies, the course is well set for Business Process Outsourcing. Accordingly, the list of companies outsourcing services of low, middle, and high complexities to the BPO stronghold India is top class. Among these companies are HSBC, CitiBank, and American Express. They are all profiting from their decision. Hardly any wonder, since the opportunities for cost-cutting are over 30%. It is no surprise then that some banks have comparatively lagged behind on the global platform and have disappeared from the leading positions on the hit list of successful credit institutes.

India is almost unbeatable in offering BPO services

India offers its potential BPO clients a unique environment. And this is not just because of the trend-setting, booming IT industry. This is the land of a highly motivated, technologically adept workforce that has mastered English almost like their mother tongue. Nowhere in the world besides in the US do so many people speak perfect English. A qualified next generation is also well taken care of. Every year, a large number of young engineers graduate from the colleges and are eager to apply their know-how in practice.

The enormous cost efficiency is a further criterion for the dynamic growth in the BPO sector. A practical example: In a call center, the personnel costs amount to 55% to 60% of the total cost – a number that would probably literally shake up a Western entrepreneur. But if he decides to outsource his services to India, his costs would drop by a tenth of what they would be in Europe.

The Indian government has recognized the opportunity of building India to a world leader in this sector and supports its development through various initiatives. »Promotion of the IT service sector« is in fact number five on the government's list of priorities. The government has eased the rules and regulations for international investors and even allows companies to be in 100% foreign ownership. An improved IT infrastructure and modern telecommunication facilities contribute to promoting sustainable growth in the sector. The development rate of the last few years is phenomenal: in 1998, close to 23,000 people were employed in this sector, generating a turnover of 10 million US dollars. Forecasts suggest that in a span of the next ten years, that is, in 2008, there will be at least a million employed in this sector, and according to the forecast of an insider, the turnover would jump to 20 billion US dollars. The current development points to this forecast being absolutely possible. The central fields of activity in future will be the back office services for credit institutes, operations in service and industry, handling of claims for insurance companies, and interaction with the clients of the international outsourcer.

Important addresses for those interested in India are:
- German Office for Foreign Trade, www.bfai.com
- Indo-German Chamber of Commerce, www.indo-german.com
- National Association of Software & Service Companies (NASSCOM), www.nasscom.org
- BPO India, www.bpoindia.org
- Banknet India, www.banknetindia.com

Sourcing market Turkey

The economic policy in Turkey is largely driven by the wish to soon be accepted in the EU. This wish is reflected in many reforms that aim to liberalize domestic and foreign trade. The economic policy is very entrepreneur-friendly. Turkey seems to have overcome the grave economic and financial crisis of 2000 and 2001, when a massive inflation rate of over 80 % and a tremendous increase in government debts led to the downfall of the economy. Since 2002, the reforms supported by the International Monetary Fund (IMF) are picking up and leading to continuous growth – around 10 % in 2004. Export is booming, inflation is clearly reducing, and the currency is gaining in strength.

The country's economy has seen a fundamental change in the last few years. Earlier, agriculture was at the center of the economy. Today, there are differentiated structures, with a clear divide between Eastern and Western Turkey. In the west of the country, industry is seeing a clear boom. This is where the textile, automobile, chemical, engineering, and electronics industries are concentrated. Agriculture is still the main occupation in the east and southeast of the country. An important reason for the same is the lack of general infrastructure in these regions. Today, although close to 40 % of the total population of 70 million works in the agricultural sector, it contributes to only 13 % of the Gross National Product (GNP). Industry, on the other hand, generates about 25 % of the GNP. The service industry, with its 62 % share in the GNP, is the largest contributor, thanks to the popularity of the country among tourists.

The continuous boom has a definite impact on the per capita income. Nevertheless, the national average, according to the World Bank, still frequently lies below the level in many developing countries. The statistic, however, does not consider the grave differences in income between the booming Western Turkey and the slowly developing Eastern Turkey.

Relations with Europe since centuries

Turkey's candidature for entry into the EU is not the only reason for the good relations and the constantly growing economic exchange between Turkey and the EU. Several institutions have taken it upon themselves to consolidate the bilateral relations. One of these is the German-Turkish cooperation council, which is engaged in topics like politics, the economy, environment, and transport and communication. Regular negotiations by the government aim at further developing the economic cooperation. The customs union that came into force in early 1996 created the necessary setting for a forced economic cooperation. A double taxation agreement between Turkey and the EU promoted bilateral economic relations as well.

Within the EU, Germany has long since been Turkey's most important trade partner – a position that experts are convinced will be further strengthened. Bilateral trade volumes in 2004 again showed a clear rise, reaching a record 20 billion euros. Turkish exports into Germany worth about 8 billion euros constituted 14 % of the total exports. The amount of goods and services exported from Germany into Turkey was close to 12 billion euros.

German companies are not only important partners of the Turkish economy but they also invest in Turkey much more than any other country does. The number of German companies that have sister concerns in Turkey is also steadily increasing. The number of German-Turkish joint ventures, too, is on the rise.

Turkey – On the way to the top of the industrial textile sector

Until recently, if anyone were asked about Turkey's most important product in terms of export, the answer would almost always have been »garments«. This was indeed true until the Chinese and the Vietnamese ousted the Turks from the top position and established themselves in this sector as the most affordable. The Turkish textile industry, however, did not spiral into depression. Instead, it is working intensively – and with growing success – on carving out a niche for itself in the textile sector and regaining its number one position, this time in the area of industrial textiles. Some examples are articles in the area of hygiene, car filters, car interiors, sieves, insulating materials, airbags, and conveyor belts.

Pronounced increase in demand in the global market

The demand for industrial textiles is rising dynamically. Until 2006 alone, the sector is expected to grow annually by 10% globally. The first to profit from this are the developing countries and emerging economies. This development can be backed by impressive figures: in 1991, North America, Europe, and Japan held about 75% of the world market. In ten years, this figure is down to 66% – in favor of the smaller countries.

Why is Turkey profiting from the development?

Employees of Kerkhoff Consulting in Istanbul researched why Turkey will be among the profit makers in the booming market of industrial textiles. As part of the research, manufacturers in Turkey were interviewed about their current situation and their plans for the future. In addition, the research also included talks with their customers and a market analysis. The result: Turkey is already an ideal sourcing market for industrial textiles today, and this position will continue to be strengthened. The country had in the past won a very good reputation for the production of felt. This know-how, along with highly skilled workers in the garments sector, fulfills the technical prerequisites. New manufacturers are focusing exclusively on high-tech production processes. It is the flexible working hours, above all, that differentiate Turkish manufacturers from those in Western Europe. Discussions on reducing working hours are unheard-of in Turkey. At the same time, the location of the country makes it possible to have quick access to buyers all over Europe. All these factors contribute to making Turkey the first address when it comes to global sourcing of industrial textiles. With an entry into the booming economic sector, international investors are allowing themselves opportunities for excellent profits, because growth in this sector will definitely continue, at least in the middle term.

Important addresses for those interested in Turkey are:
- German Office for Foreign Trade, www.bfai.com
- Turkish-German Chamber of Commerce and Industry, www.dtr-ihk.de
- Under secretariat of Turkish Prime Ministry for Foreign Trade, http://www.dtm.gov.tr/engmenu.htm Export Promotion Center, http://www.igeme.org.tr/introeng.htm
- Price Waterhouse Coopers – Turkey, http://www.pwcglobal.com/tr/eng/main/home/
- The Union of Chambers and Commodity Exchanges of Turkey, http://www.tobb.org.tr/eng/index.php
- World Bank Europe and Central Asia, Turkey, http://www.worldbank.org.tr/

Sourcing market Eastern Europe

On May 1, 2004, Poland, Hungary, the Czech Republic, Slovakia, Slovenia, Estonia, Latvia, and Lithuania joined the EU. This gave rise to the largest single market in the West – comprising more than 450 billion people and generating a Gross Domestic Product of almost 9 billion euros. It is not just the entry into the EU, however, that brought these Eastern European accession countries to the attention of business enterprises interested in sustainable growth.

Since decades, this region has been a very attractive sourcing market, and trade with Eastern Europe has been increasing with every year. The eagerness to purchase among the 75 million people of the new Eastern European EU states is rising with the growing strength of their economy.

It is already clear that the accession countries will profit in the long term from this development. Improved access to modern technology has proven to be a great help in raising the productivity, and Western direct investments are bringing the necessary capital into the region. Besides, entry into the EU also means access to aid money for building up and strengthening the economic and social infrastructure. An interesting aspect for Western companies eager to invest in this region.

The general conditions available for business in Eastern Europe are above average: the wages are well below Western standards, and the forecasts, too, point to further growth. Purchasing power is increasing, and the currency is stable. These are reasons enough for the rapid pace at which companies of all sizes from the West are making a beeline for this region. Especially the automobile industry has discovered the region as an attractive sourcing market and production location. For example, Audi manufactures in Hungary, Porsche buys car bodies from Slovakia, and Volkswagen has production facilities in various locations in the Eastern European EU countries. Isuzu, one of the oldest automotive companies in Japan, had its diesel engine plants begin production in Poland in 1999. The Korean automobile giant Hyundai has a manufacturing plant at Izmir Alikhya in Turkey.

The accession countries have become very important trade partners because of the constantly upward trend of their economies. This is the reason why even large international trade groups are consolidating their presence in Eastern Europe. The opportunities of sustainable profitable growth look good. One of the factors is that concentration in trade is less developed here as compared to countries of the West. The other is the fact that these markets are far from saturated, and therefore further positive development is foreseeable. With increasing wages the purchasing power, too, will rise, which will have a positive impact on the demand for foreign goods.

We present here the economic situation in the important Eastern European EU accession countries:

Poland

The Polish economy has shown an impressive change since the start of the transformation process. In many areas, practically Western structures are already present. The gross value added in the service sector is over 50%, while it is just about 24% in industry. The figures for the construction sector and agriculture are 7% and just under 3%, respectively. Much more than half the value added is generated by private enterprises that employ 70% of the total workforce. Dynamically growing exports, a steady boom in industrial production, and constantly increasing investments drive the positive economic development of the country forward. Food production, energy supply, mining, and the metallurgical industry are at the top of the list of important industries, followed by engineering and electronics industry, vehicle construction, textiles, and garments. With a population of 38 million, Poland is the largest market among all EU accession countries. This, in addition to favourable investment conditions, has managed to exert a great pull on foreign investors. Poland trades primarily with developed countries, to which it sends 74.8% of all exported goods. In 2003 trade with the EU accounted for 69% of all Polish exports and 61% of Polish imports. In 2003 Poland increased its exports mainly to Sweden, Italy, the Czech Republic, Ukraine, France, Great Britain and the Netherlands. Increased imports are observed from China, the Czech Republic, Italy, France and Germany. Among developing countries, South African trade with Poland accounts for over 100 million US dollars worth of goods and services. South Africa is among the first 5 African countries doing business with Poland. Trade is steadily increasing between the two countries with South Africa enjoying a positive balance of trade.

Important addresses for those interested in Poland are:
- German Office for Foreign Trade, www.bfai.com
- Polish-German Chamber of Commerce and Industry, www.ihk.pl

- Poland Portal, www.poland.gov.pl
- Polish Information and Foreign Investment Agency, www.paiz.gov.pl
- Warsaw Voice-Daily information about Poland, www.warsawvoice.pl
- Polish Yellow Pages, www.yellowpages.pl

Czech Republic

A good climate for consumption, strong exports, and high invest-ments from foreign investors are the factors responsible for steady growth in the Czech Republic. More than half the industrial produc-tion today comes from the factories of foreign investors. These com-panies also account for some 70% of the total exports. This is the reason the government is attracting more foreign direct investments by introducing promotional programs and by supporting the com-panies in their export efforts. The longstanding economic relations between Germany and the Czech Republic have in fact further im-proved after its entry into the EU. EU exports to the Czech Republic rose by over 15% in 2004, while imports from the Czech Republic increased by some 22%.

Important addresses for those interested in the Czech Republic are:
- German Office for Foreign Trade, www.bfai.com
- Czech-German Chamber of Commerce and Industry, www.dtihk.cz
- Portal Czech Republic Online, www.tschechien-online.org
- Czech Republic Information, www.czechcentrum.cz
- Investment and Business Development Agency, www.czechinvest.org
- Czech Business Web Portal, www.businessinfo.cz
- National Trade Promotion Agency, www.czechtradeoffices.com
- Czech Commercial Search Engine (offers and inquires mar-ket), www.abc.cz

Hungary

The Hungarian economy has been on a steady rise for many years now. A major factor in this development has been the export of the industry modernized by Western investors. Many international companies have invested in Hungary, such as Audi, Telekom, E-ON, Allianz, Bosch, and Carl Zeiss. Medium-sized companies, too, especially those in the automobile industry and engineering industry, have their own production facilities in the country. According to a survey conducted by the German-Hungarian Chamber of Commerce and Industry, over 80% of all German investors said they were »very satisfied« with their business commitments in Hungary. The good relations between the two countries are also reflected in the bilateral trade: Germany has been for many years now Hungary's most important business partner.

Important addresses for those interested in Hungary are:
- German Office for Foreign Trade, www.bfai.com
- German-Hungarian Chamber of Commerce and Industry, www.duihk.hu
- Hungarian Investment and Trade Development Agency, www.itd.hu
- Ministry of Economy and Transport, Republic of Hungary, www.gkm.gov.hu

Romania, on the way to becoming an attractive sourcing market

It is not just the Eastern European EU countries that have excellent conditions for procurement and that offer high-value products. Romania is fast becoming a very attractive sourcing market. This is particularly true in the areas of automobiles, information and communications technology, engineering and plant construction, chemicals and pharmaceuticals, furniture, textiles, and food processing. The planned construction of railways, harbor facilities, and power plants with the help of international financial institutions and the EU will further promote the positive development of the country. Economic growth in 2004 was well above 8 %. Experts are convinced that this trend will continue in the next few years. A broad program for reforms shall prepare the country and its 22 million inhabitants for entry into the EU. Essential initiatives of the reforms program are measures like reducing taxes, fighting corruption, and dealing with the parallel economy. The EU has officially recognized the success already achieved by the country.

Trade relations between Romania and Western countries are developing dynamically. Italian products accounted for around 25 % of the 20 billion US dollars worth of overall imports into Romania in 2004, making Italy Romania's leading business partner. The relationship is two-way, since Italy is also the leading export market for Romanian industries. This, then, is also an opportunity to contribute to development of this country, in which construction activity is developing at a growing rate and where the quality and technology of Italian products may once meet with success.

Some voices in the industry are going as far as to call Romania, in particular, an upcoming »outsourcing rival« to India. Costs are still very low, education levels are high, science and engineering graduates are readily available, and cultural affinity with the West is greater than that of India with excellent foreign language skills (and the flights are much shorter). The average gross wage per month in Romania is currently reported at 328.76 US dollars (including taxes).

Important addresses for those interested in Romania are:
- German Office for Foreign Trade, www.bfai.com
- German-Romanian Chamber of Commerce and Industry, www.ahk-germany.de/rumaenien
- Trade Romania Directory, www.trade-romania.biz
- Foreign Trade Promotion Center, www. aneir-cpce.ro
- Romanian Company Database, www.romanian-companies.ro
- Regional Chamber of Commerce, www.region-one-chamber.ro
- The Chamber of Commerce & Industry of Romania, www.ccir.ro
- Romania Factbook 2005, Trade Regulations, Customs & Standards,

www.factbook.net/countryreports/ro/Ro_TradeRegs.htm
- Romanian Company Database, www.listafirme.ro
- B2B Portal, www.ghidafaceri.ro
- National Bank of Romania, www.bnr.ro
- Profit Romania, B2B E-Market Place, www.profitromania.com
- Business Online, www.b2b-bestof.com/retailers/romania_
  yellow_pages

Chapter 4
Global Sourcing as a Profit Booster

Global sourcing makes international procurement a strategic element of the corporate strategy of any future-oriented company just as much as local or domestic sourcing. Jacek Wojtasik, Managing Director and owner of Karina Meble, a trading and consulting company for office furnishing is also convinced. »There have been great changes in the international procurement markets in the last few years. Quality, security of supply and logistic costs are the main factors used in evaluating foreign markets and suppliers. The dynamics of this situation necessitates constant observation of ongoing economic and technological developments. A strategic approach can help a company to set up a global structure of suppliers and improve it's profit potential, thereby also enhancing its position in the competitive market.«

The implementation of an effective global sourcing strategy is not fundamentally different from the institutionalizing of strategic procurement activities in the surrounding area of the company. It is important, however, to consider the varying general conditions, as well as the higher complexity of some aspects, that decide the sustainable success of global sourcing.

Some of these aspects are:
- The structures of foreign markets are, to an extent, very different. So are the mentalities and business miens of international suppliers.
- Procuring the necessary information can be time-consuming and expensive because of various possible communication problems, like difficulties with the language, the great distance from the sourcing market, or different notions of quality.
- Buyers and technicians may have some reservations about foreign products, based either on unpleasant experiences or on

friendly relations, going back many years, with national suppliers.
- The information about the situation in the particular market may be insufficient or totally absent.

These aspects not only underline the importance of formulating global sourcing as one of the many criterions of the purchasing department, but also progressively make international procurement the focus. This is the only way to realize sustainable success of the strategy and to generate long-term profit potential for your company. For years, the 28.2 billion dollars United Technologies Corp. (UTC) has acted primarily as a holding company for its subsidiaries – Carrier, Hamilton Sundstrand, Otis, Pratt & Whitney, Sikorsky Aircraft and UTC Power – with offices in nearly 180 countries. Each subsidiary had its own enterprise systems, processes for sourcing projects and IT organizational structures. UTC continues to function as a holding company, but it also provides support for its subsidiaries for common business processes such as HR and indirect sourcing. In 2001, Chairman and CEO George David decided that it was high time for UTC to reap some benefits from the combined size and power of its companies. He issued a decree for UTC to squeeze 500 million dollars out of its annual 3.5 billion dollars direct procurement costs. Doucette, who had just been promoted to CIO of UTC, was responsible for 40 million dollars of the mandated savings.

On the following pages, you will experience, in detail, which activities are essential to make global sourcing a profit booster for companies. Among these are the targeted choice of the products to be procured abroad, the choice of the international sourcing market, seeking and assessing potential suppliers, and the formulation of a convincing request for proposal. In addition, it is important to analyze the potential supplier in his own country, to get acquainted with their individual way of carrying out negotiations, and to react to the same with a target-orientated approach. If one wishes to succeed at global sourcing in the long run, it is necessary to carry out operative supplier management and controlling and adapt the organization of one's purchasing department to the new requirements. Although this will lengthen the installation process, it is well worth it, according to Dr. Günter Scheipermeier, Managing Director of the renowned fitted kitchen manufacturer Nobilia-Werke J. Stickling GmbH & Co. He explains, »Global sourcing cannot be implemented in a lightning-quick process, which is the reason why we gave ourselves the necessary time, and today we can reap the fruits of strategic international procurement. We are seeing an increase in the value added, despite massive price pressure.«

Which products are suitable for global sourcing?

International procurement will lead to the desired success to a large extend if the individual parts or complete products fulfill the following prerequisites. If some criteria are not applicable, more traditional ways of procurement can be pursued. It is, however, important to inform your available suppliers that you are intensively working with the issue of global sourcing. By doing so, often one comes across a far non-existing readiness to negotiate among the national suppliers.

1. High proportion of labor costs

In industrialized countries, products that are personnel cost intensive are unavoidably expensive. Making use of the lower labor costs in emerging economies is the most crucial reason for undertaking international procurement. In principle, one should exercise caution and conduct a detailed analysis of markets. If the sourcing country, in turn, procures the necessary raw material abroad, it can quickly put the advantage of labor costs in perspective. It is important to consider this point of view before reaching a decision on the sourcing country.

2. Average technological and qualitative requirements

In the initial phase, it is advisable for the company to restrict itself to parts that can be manufactured without requiring any complex production processes or particular know-how. It is best to exercise caution, even when the new supplier assures excellent product characteristics and presents the corresponding sample parts. Many emerging economies have a very different understanding of quality, making fluctuations in quality is not too uncommon. It has almost become a rule to conduct regular product tests in the country of manufacture, even in case of longstanding partnerships.

3. High procurement volumes

There are no fixed limits set for the possible order quantity per product. Experience shows, however, that an order volume upwards of 500,000 euros is common for efficient international procurement for newcomers who begin with procuring only one product abroad. Only by doing so can the necessary costs (travel costs, research costs, interpreter's fee, additional expenses for research and development, production, and technology, transportation costs, and controlling costs) be balanced with the targeted benefit. If, however, a company already has experience in global sourcing, and if it knows several efficient and reliable suppliers, then it can negotiate attractive conditions even for smaller quantities.

4. Low complexity of materials

Especially in China, materials of the required quality are not always available. In such cases, the suppliers resort to using other materials of inferior quality. This risk can be reduced only when close business relations with reliable companies have been built. And this would take a certain amount of time, as in the local market. It could make good business sense, in some cases, to procure the raw material locally and send it to the sourcing country for processing – for example, in the manufacture of high-value tools. This is how the producer of cosmetic packaging Heinz Plastics Poland has, meanwhile, been procuring a part of its requirement in Romania. To ensure quality in series production, raw materials are supplied from certified suppliers of first-class quality. One week after the necessary drawings have reached Romania, the offer is tendered by the alternative supplier. Success for Heinz Plastics: as compared to the conventional process, the company realizes savings of as much as 40% through global sourcing.

5. Possibility of planning the required quantity

China and India are thousands of kilometers away from Europe, which leads to long shipment times (China: minimum 30 days, India: 20 to 30 days). Loading and unloading the ships and the final transport to the buyer from the port adds to the actual transportation time. Times have changed from when one could simply call up and order the goods that one needed in a few hours time. An annual detailed plan that should be coordinated with suppliers and logistics companies is the order of the day. Companies that can offer potential suppliers precise data improve their negotiating position. In addition to this, if the buyer needs to procure a large quantity of goods internationally, his negotiating position naturally improves. The effects of grouping along with the lowering of the price margins are of great use.

6. Multiple suppliers

Depending on just one supplier harbors more risks in global sourcing, as compared to traditional sourcing. The product that you would like to procure internationally should therefore be capable of being manufactured without any problems, that is, without a long test phase. It is therefore not recommended to work with just one supplier from a country, rather to identify potential partners in a wide region who are in a position to deliver on short notice. This reduces the supply risks that could arise after signing the contract and ensures supply in times of strikes, political unrest, and natural catastrophes.

7. Clarity of drawings and technical specifications

It has been a long time since all companies have had complete product specifications. Often the information and drawings are decades old. It is likely that those who wish to source globally want to update their specifications, adapt them to international norms, and perhaps even translate them into the local language of the sourcing country. The simpler and clearer the drawings and technical specifications, the better is the supplied quality. Further cumbersome communication can thus be avoided.

8. Small proportion of transportation costs / High shelf life and transportability

Foodstuff, above all, requires elaborate storage because of its perishable nature and usually needs further processing quickly. These requirements are definitely reflected in the storage and transportation costs. Dispatch of goods also proves to be a cost driver, especially in case of products requiring particularly complex packaging. It therefore makes more sense for a European buyer to restrict himself to suppliers from relatively nearer regions like Poland, Romania, or Turkey, or to continue procuring from the available suppliers. In extreme cases, the storage and transportation costs can exceed the favorable labor costs in the sourcing country. Products that are considered for global sourcing should therefore have a long shelf life and good transportability. The basic principle that the total costs of global sourcing should be well under the costs of national or regional sourcing also applies here.

9. Low import duties

It is important for those interested in global sourcing to consider the duty regulations while deciding for a suitable sourcing country. Normally, import duties seldom lie above 5% or 10% of the product price. However, there are countries which enter into so-called preferential agreements with their outsourcing partners, which facilitate lower rates of duty or the absence of them altogether. Such advantages could be essential decisive factors because often the cost savings at the product level are sapped by the rates of duty.

Is your purchasing department correctly positioned for global sourcing?

Western companies are slowly beginning to discover the high significance of the purchasing department in achieving profitable growth and for the return into the profit zone. In many companies, however, the purchasing department continues to have a very low significance and is not accepted by other departments as an equal partner. This is the reason why some purchasing organizations restrict themselves to being exclusively operational in their activity and initialize order processes only mechanically, instead of actively contributing towards increasing the profit of the company. It is only seldom that these buyers invite offers from other suppliers and conduct strategic procurement management focused on sustainable increase in profit. Often, the question of whether strategic procurement management is part of the applied instruments is answered in the negative. It is not just that the purchasing managers hardly have an idea of what the term means. Very often, the people we spoke to even had an unsatisfactory basic understanding of the business model of their own company, its vision, and strategic direction. In such a scenario, it is impossible to carry out efficient procurement management, let alone using global sourcing to one's benefit.

The essential reason why strategic procurement and international sourcing have become the order of the day is the completely changed set of requirements confronting purchasing departments today. The rapidly developing globalization is leading to an aggressive price competition, which organizations can only survive if they utilize all their untapped potential in the area of procurement. At the same time, the disappearing national borders are offering the opportunity to cooperate with suppliers that are very convincing with their high-quality products at unrivalled prices. To be able to profit from these new sources of procurement in the long term, the employees in the purchasing department need to study the global sourcing market up to the last detail and search for new trends and developments with the help of modern tools. This gives the purchasing department a hitherto almost unknown significance. This development is quite a culture shock for many traditional buyers. They should, however, adapt to the new situation and discard the habit of essentially functioning only operationally. A practical example shows with just how much business sense the official hand continues to operate in the area of procurement. A consultant succeeded in identifying a cost-cutting volume of an impressive 80% for a product that was to be procured annually for 4 billion euros. The concerned authority, however, did not take the suggestion and continued to procure according to the traditional method and that with chronically empty cash registers.

Operational procurement – An unavoidable routine

What is meant by operational procurement, without which a purchasing department naturally cannot function successfully? Here is the explanation: operational procurement is one of the less-loved routine functions, with which many buyers often spend or rather waste – a large part of their working time. Among these unavoidable tasks are the formulation of inquiries, detailing individual and general agreements, data administration, and order processing. Experience shows that many companies frequently use completely antiquated procedures for these activities, which in effect are enormously time-consuming and unnecessarily block the buyers' capacities. Tending to the existing suppliers, negotiating with them, and carrying out quality assurance are other activities among the spectrum of tasks in the area of operational procurement. These activities are recurring and do not challenge the buyers enough over a period of time. Reorganizing these processes can, on an average, save up to 50% time. Not just that: process costs, too, can be brought down by up to 30%. The newly created capacities of the buyers can be used for strategic procurement and the costs saved definitely improve the result.

Strategic procurement management – Basis for profitable growth

Times have changed since a company could afford to procure exclusively on the spur of the moment, that is, order only to meet a current demand. If a buyer continues to restrict himself to operational activities, he will only tend to do more damage to his employer than good. Today, purchasing departments should work at creating global transparency and get well versed with national and international sourcing markets.

This means that buyers need to get rid of many dear habits. Among these is the longstanding cooperation with suppliers without regularly making sure that their prices and conditions are actually competitive. This could cause many well-established relationships between buyers and suppliers to fall apart, because, in practice, it is experienced often that those buyers who blindly trust partners and believe that they are being offered the best prices frequently get deceived.

In addition to global sourcing, a whole lot of other tools are important for modern strategic procurement management. Some of these may already be known and possibly, also used. It is worth getting to know and to use these instruments. To do so successfully, however, it is important to train the buyers and prepare them for the new challenges.

Here is a short definition of the essential success factors of the reorientation of procurement:

- *Procurement planning and control:* Key figures fulfill the prerequisites for steering procurement on the basis of profit-oriented data and identifying successes or failures. Only those who plan the key figures and define them as a goal can steer them. It is important to analyze whether there are any planned figures in your purchasing organization. Are your purchasing managers appraised on the basis of achieved success and paid accordingly? Experience shows that there is an abundance of untapped potential in many companies in this area.
- *Sourcing market research:* Significant procedures make it possi-

ble to analyze differentiated information on available supplier potential, the current situation of competition, qualifications of possible suppliers, and their conduct while dealing with customers. Market research in the area of procurement should be made systematically. As naturally as this tool is implemented in marketing for identifying customer requirements, it is surprising that one finds it in the smallest of companies, not just in global sourcing market research. Confront your supplier with questions on sourcing market research. Only a supplier that systematically analyzes markets, competitors, suppliers, value chains, and business models is capable of procuring correctly.

– *Make or buy:* A company's decision to make or buy has a close connection with the optimization of the own operational value added and therefore, inevitably with a related increase in the external procurement costs. As illustrated in our case studies in chapter 2, Bree and H&M are classic examples of make or buy decisions. The own value added is clearly reduced. The correct shift to international suppliers increases the competitiveness and significantly reduces costs simultaneously.

– *Total cost of ownership:* This strategic procurement management tool makes sure that there is an overall understanding and a corresponding transparency of all costs accompanying the procurement of products and services. Besides the direct costs, many indirect costs that are connected to procurement, maintenance, repair, use, etc. of the products, also flow in. This approach also attempts to calculate and control costs connected with the life cycle of the product *(product life cycle costing)*. This concept is explained in detail in the context of material group analysis, which is of great significance in the framework of global sourcing.

– *Concept competitions:* At internal workshops, potential suppliers have the opportunity to present their ideas along with the initial broad calculation of costs, before a committee of potential buyers. López put it across at Volkswagen. Concept competitions not only assure the required quality early, but they also automatically initiate a competition between suppliers and maintain the costs within certain prescribed limits.

- *Simultaneous engineering:* At the core of this strategy is the close cooperation between all concerned departments while developing a product and while planning the production process – from R&D, quality assurance, and finance, right up to production, marketing and sales, logistics, and, naturally, procurement. The supplier is an integral part of the product development process. His early involvement in turn ensures quality and maintenance of the cost limit. Even if simultaneous engineering, that is developing products mutually with selected suppliers, cannot per se accompany global sourcing, however it is an important strategy for international procurement. It is, therefore, clear from the outset which product components are fundamental for the final development. The company and its suppliers can decide, regarding the choice of preliminary suppliers, what is to be procured nationally or internationally without watering down the core of the product in the process.
- *Target costing:* Often, the concept of target costing is paraphrased as an integrated cost management concept for planning, supervision, and control of all cost structures. Primarily, this tool serves to influence the product costs at an early stage of development. The most important question at the outset is how much the customer is prepared to pay for the product or service. This means that the cost management concept is strictly market oriented. Target costing integrates all functions of the company, including the supplier. This is controlled by a strict supplier cost engineering, which details which supplier will supply what product at what price, and also where the supplier is located. Intelligent target costing looks at global sourcing as a significant element in maintaining the limits of target costs.
- *Value analysis:* This process aims at reducing the costs of a product or its components, while still maintaining its functions and characteristics. Besides, value analysis makes it possible to incorporate changes that will increase the value of the product. Value analysis will be discussed in detail in the actual process of global sourcing, because it plays a role in deciding where specific product parts and components should be procured.

- *Benchmarking:* In close connection with the efforts of companies to achieve the best possible price for the product or service to be procured are the comparisons with the competition, known as »benchmarking.« It is a structured process for identifying the potential for improvement and comprehensive change, and implementing the same. Especially with global sourcing, perfectly applicable benchmarking should be the order of the day. Only when one regularly compares suppliers, regardless of whether they are national or international, can the best possible price-to-performance ratio be realized during procurement.

Before you begin developing the purchasing department to a significant generator of success, you should be clear of the overall strategy followed by your company. The procurement strategy should be oriented accordingly. Do you want to capture new markets, or do you want to strengthen your position as a leader in technology? Does it involve restructuring, or is it exclusively about increasing the profit?

Self-test: How well is your purchasing organization positioned?

The following statements will tell you in minutes whether your organization is already efficiently positioned to be a purchasing organization, and whether it is in a position to successfully source abroad. Please answer the statements with »yes« or »no«:

	Yes (1)	No (0)
1. Our purchasing department is headed by a strategically acting purchasing manager.		
2. The employees spend over 50% of their time looking into strategic questions.		
3. The responsibilities in our purchasing department are clearly and precisely regulated.		
4. The purchasing organization is organized in consistence with national and international procurement.		
5. Over 40% of our procurement volume is already sourced internationally.		
6. Our purchasing department consists of a sourcing market research section comprising several people.		
7. Many buyers know our company due to longstanding activities in other functions.		
8. Every buyer exactly knows our business strategy.		
9. The purchasing department orients its strategy to the overall corporate strategy.		
10. Our purchasing organization perfectly covers the global sourcing market in terms of language.		
11. The employees are aware of the value of global sourcing.		
12. The purchasing department acts as an interface between the other departments in the company.		

	Yes (1)	No (0)
13. Communication with other departments is regulated in a clear and understandable manner.		
14. The purchasing department is consistently integrated with product development.		
15. The purchasing department openly communicates the conditions of the suppliers to the relevant departments in the company.		
16. We carry out an active supplier benchmarking that constantly compares existing and new suppliers.		
17. All departments are aware why international suppliers are substituting national suppliers.		
18. The purchasing department decides which products are inquired about nationally and which internationally.		
19. The buyers travel within their sourcing markets at least three days every week.		
20. Our sourcing market research goes beyond purely secondary information, for example, from the Internet.		
21. The national supplier selection process follows a strict procedure that is known to everyone in the company.		
22. The international supplier selection process follows a strict procedure that is known to everyone in the company.		
23. Criteria for selecting national and international suppliers are clearly and precisely defined.		

	Yes (1)	No (0)
24. We permanently conduct concept competitions in cooperation with the purchasing department as well as research and development (R&D).		
25. We have a clear understanding which suppliers are important to us.		
26. We know exactly which products and parts can be procured globally.		
27. The purchasing department decides which products should be procured globally from how many suppliers.		
28. Our buyers always conduct product value analyses – often, together with R&D and the production department.		
29. Total cost of ownership is an instrument used by our buyers to globally assess suppliers.		
30. An active material group management decides which products should be procured globally.		
31. The buyers group together requirement volumes according to business areas, international subsidiaries, location, brands, etc.		
32. The purchasing department is exactly aware of the competitive position of the suppliers.		
33. Our purchasing department can relate to the calculations of the suppliers.		
34. The buyers are exactly aware of the global price development in the most important material groups.		
35. Quality problems with our national suppliers can be promptly identified.		

	Yes (1)	No (0)
36. Supply problems with our international suppliers can be promptly identified.		
37. In the framework of global sourcing, the processes are audited at the supplier's place of business itself.		
38. There is a clear regulation about which supplier will support our company technically and logistically on location.		
39. Our purchasing department has developed a detailed supplier assessment system that considers many strategic approaches, like value analysis, target costing, etc.		
40. The supplier assessments are conducted by a team from the departments of purchasing, R&D, production, and controlling, principally every quarter.		
41. The consequences of a bad supplier assessment are clearly defined for the supplier.		
42. Our purchasing department guarantees that there is no drain of know-how to the suppliers due to global sourcing.		
43. Global sourcing has a high value in our company.		
44. Our buyers are, at this stage, regularly sourcing in Eastern Europe.		
45. Our buyers are, at this stage, regularly sourcing in India.		
46. Our buyers are, at this stage, regularly sourcing in China.		

	Yes (1)	No (0)
47. We have a formulated process and course of action for global sourcing.		
48. Our management/our board of directors can be appraised on the basis of success in global sourcing.		
49. Global sourcing is a top management task in our company.		
50. We have clearly defined who should be involved in the global sourcing decision while procuring a product.		
51. Our purchasing department processes knowledge on international contract law.		
52. Negotiations with international suppliers are conducted regularly in the respective country.		
53. Our purchasing department negotiates to push through further price concessions, even during the course of the contract.		
54. Products to be procured globally are so specified that they can be ordered from various international suppliers at any time.		
55. Our decentralized buyers regularly coordinate their respective sourcing requirements.		

Evaluation:

For every »yes,« you get one point, for every »no,« zero points.

55 to 46 points: An excellent result. The purchasing organization largely corresponds to the requirements of a modern procurement management. The advantages of global sourcing, too, are known, and the company has experience in this area. You are on the right path. But you have not yet tapped the full potential. Carry on consistently, and discuss with your concerned employees what can be done so that the statements in the self-test that were answered with a »no« could be answered in the future with a »yes.« By doing so, you will clearly set the course for sustainable growth of profits.

45 to 35 points: A satisfactory result. In your company, global sourcing enjoys a higher priority than in many other companies. You are aware of the modern tools of a profit-oriented procurement. Clarify with your buyers whether they actually master these instruments and use them satisfactorily. The same applies to global sourcing. You can and should work more efficiently in this area. It is best to start immediately and make your procurement a significant profit booster for your company.

34 to 10 points: Unfortunately, an unsatisfactory result. Modern procurement management and global sourcing seem to be foreign words for at least some of your buyers. It is therefore high time to start taking action if you do not wish to risk being relegated to the league of losers in this day of extreme competition. There is an acute need for further training. There are a lot of technical literature and seminars available to help counterbalance the deficits. There is a great likelihood that you would need to completely restructure your procurement. Therefore, consult experts in the field.

9 to 0 points: Alert phase one. Your procurement continues to be largely restricted to functioning operationally. This could be justified by the low value this department enjoys and the resulting lack of motivation among the buyers. It is now important to make a new beginning as early as possible. Many sources of profit have been left untapped until now. In the worst case, the company runs the risk of making losses.

Hardly any company is achieving optimum results today in the area of procurement management. There is a lot to be done, otherwise there is the risk of losing out to international competition, at least in the long run.

Comprehensive data collection – Clear decision for or against global sourcing

Global sourcing is one of the significant success tools of future-oriented companies that aim for sustainable profitable growth and wish to clearly differentiate themselves from their competitors. It has already been explained on the earlier pages that high transportation costs, or necessary costs for quality assurance, for example, can well exceed the achievable cost-cutting potential. A three-tier process helps reach a decision on whether it really makes business sense to procure a product or material abroad. It begins with product value analysis and material group analysis. The final tier is cost analysis.

1. Product value analysis

When it comes to making regular orders with suppliers, many traditionally oriented buyers react rather mechanically and perform only the necessary formalities. The result: the same, often unnecessary and expensive materials continue to be used, and elaborate production procedures that are possibly already outdated are applied. A product value analysis does not just stop this waste of money. It offers much more: the process creates the basis to ensure that the specified characteristics and functions of the product are maintained; in some cases, in fact, they are optimized – in spite of convincing reduction in costs. In addition, one can save time and resources. The purchasing department cannot single-handedly bring about such positive effects. The departments of research and development, production, storage, sales, and service should support it. The early integration of suppliers is also possible. However it should be in connection with the product, component, or system to be analyzed.

At the joint coordination meetings attended by representatives of the departments and from various hierarchical levels, the respective product is analyzed in detail and creative possibilities for improvement are sought. This is how the strategically important components can be separated from the parts that are easily replaceable by others during production. Often, these articles with strategically lesser significance are procured at lower costs with the help of global sourcing than through the traditional method of procurement.

The product value analysis can also be used as a reliable instrument to replace the overpriced components, which were identified during target costing, with new solutions that are more efficient from a technological and business perspective.

Nevertheless, in the face of various cost-cutting possibilities through creative product value analyses, it is imperative not to forget that each product has a certain level of sensibility. This level, when crossed, reduces the value of the article for the consumer and correspondingly reduces its attractiveness.

External experts often come across tremendous opposition while attempting to implement product value analyses. One doesn't like to be separated from tried and tested products parts. Often it is noticed that, although the product value analysis by itself is seen positively, it is frequently confused or jumbled with so-called standardization approaches. Standardization projects are all about harmonizing, that is, standardizing similar products or material groups that are procured from different locations. For example, it is common in the automobile industry, where one and the same platform of the chassis is fitted in various models. The platform by itself is standardized and is therefore capable of being grouped together across various locations and application areas. Cost advantages are achievable. Standardization, then, has only an indirect relation to the value analysis. The value analysis and standardization processes should always be externally neutrally moderated. Very often, we experience that the instruments are wrongly understood. Sometimes, the feeling of this being the last time that one has the opportunity to influence the design of the product takes the front seat. The potential cost-cutting effect is quickly forgotten and the configuration of the product suffers at the hands of an ego play between the technicians. The identification of globally procurable components is, in this way, watered down, and the process of global sourcing comes to an end, even before it has actually begun.

2. Material group analysis

In practice, this process is conducted parallel, or complementary to product value analysis. Here, too, the aim is to decide which material groups are suited to global sourcing. Experience shows that many of the procured material groups are, indeed, well suited to global sourcing. This means that one can easily dispense with comprehensive value analyses. Besides, the R&D need not be convinced of the fact that a part of the product is to be procured in China or India. The company can act directly. Approximately at least 10% to 20% of the material groups that are procured by companies are sourced directly in Eastern Europe, India, or China. The identification of these 10% to 20% naturally requires some spadework. This unfortunately deters many purchasing managers. As is often the case, they do not want to change something that is tried and tested. In addition, they do not even have recourse to the technical operational departments. Often the power base of the engineers is so large, and the skepticism against foreign suppliers and their abilities are so great, that »global sourcing« approaches of procurement are simply nipped in the bud. This is why global sourcing should become an issue for the management and the board of directors. Only by doing so can awareness in the various departments and complete support of the purchasing department be developed. This can be illustrated by an example from the electronics industry. Within the framework of a material group analysis, global sourcing experts identified products that were capable of being procured globally on an immediate basis. These parts were earlier procured regionally and then further processed in presumably affordable cottage industries. Through global sourcing it was possible to not just procure these products at a much cheaper price, but also to find a foreign supplier who would undertake all the further processing – a double cost saving for our clients!

But just how are material group analyses conducted? The first step in this process is a pragmatic ABC analysis. It is de facto an instrument that can be implemented universally for the separation of particularly significant material groups (e.g., key raw materials) from material groups with lesser significance. It is used mainly for quantity-value-relations. As a rule, material groups with lesser significance that are identified within the framework of the ABC analysis are particularly suited for global sourcing – assuming that the volume is satisfactory. It is important, at this juncture, to be warned against an over-pragmatic quantity-related application. The combination with corresponding relations that are value related, above all, gives certainty of the material groups that can be globally procured. You could, for example, procure, on a value basis (value/piece), a large quantity of material groups with completely lesser significance. The large volume would bring you to the conclusion that it is, indeed, a significant material group that should be procured nationally. Global sourcing, however, can save some 10 to 15 percentage points. This is naturally insignificant in the value per piece. In the quantity required for production, however, it could make an enormous difference. The XYZ analysis is normally recommended for material group analysis. It facilitates the classification of material groups. The classification follows consumption behavior. Generally, three consumption classes are defined and differentiated. The X class signifies a constant consumption of material, accompanied by a high degree of exactness of forecast. The Y class stands for a trend-driven and seasonal consumption, with a corresponding medium degree of exactness of forecast. Z classifies material groups with an irregular consumption and an extremely low degree of exactness of forecast. Material groups of the X class are literally predestined for global sourcing. These materials are constantly required in the organization and are therefore a sort of a recurring, frequently procured material group in the purchasing organization. There are experience values of any kind, for example, the efficiency of the supplier, market and price developments, and so on, so that even a potential advantage through global sourcing can be quickly quantified. If the ABC and XYZ analyses are conducted and different material groups are identified as suitable for global sourcing, you could go through a first catalog of questions in order to further isolate the materials that are really suitable for being sourced globally.

Some of these questions are:
- *Are the products critical or uncritical?* This decision should be taken after working closely with the technicians of the company. However, these employees often react very reluctantly

when they are informed that the idea of procuring material from abroad is being considered for the future. A close involvement in the decision-making process helps in most cases, to get rid of some reservations. After all, the know-how of the research and development and the production departments should by no means remain untapped.

- *Which logistical requirements need to be taken care of?* It is important to determine whether the restrained shelf life or the dimensions and weight of the product possibly necessitate elaborate logistical measures. If there are requirements for just-in-time, it does not mean that the product is not suitable for global sourcing. It only means that intermediate stores need to be set up to further guarantee the production process.
- *Are there particular import regulations for the concerned products, and how high are the rates of duty?* Global sourcing for one or several material groups could be unattractive due to certain bureaucratic conditions and high custom duty.
- *Can the required quantities be well planned?* The same that applies to local sourcing holds true for global sourcing as well: The larger the order volumes, the more generous are the suppliers in offering concessions in the conditions and prices.

The decision for or against global sourcing of a product within the framework of a material group analysis is, therefore, dependent on various criteria, which should finally be complemented by a detailed cost analysis with the help of total cost of ownership.

3. Total cost of ownership

In the past, the effective price was the most important factor on which many buyers based their decision. But times have changed. Meanwhile, total cost of ownership (TCO) has grown to become a very important criterion in the question of cost. This process covers all costs for the product, right from the development phase up to recycling, and considers the entire life cycle, besides the price of the goods. As a result of this system, suppliers who offer products at prices higher than their competitors still have an absolutely good chance of bagging the order – especially when such suppliers offer attractive supply intervals, thereby helping the buyer to reduce his capital lockup and save on storage costs. That is, he delivers just-in-time. Just-in-time also works for global sourcing, for example, when the supplier is ready to set up a consignment stock for his customer. The buyer can draw out goods from this stock based on his need and only then does he have to pay for them. This is how, in practice, higher product prices are entirely compensated by saving on additional costs.

Principally, the approach of total cost of ownership for global sourcing should consider aspects of the entire life cycle of a product or service. Nevertheless, we would like to focus on the additional costs arising through global sourcing, or costs that arise in another form. Finally, strategic global procurement pays only if the total savings are significantly higher than the costs for international procurement. It should, after all, prove to be much cheaper to procure globally than within the region.

The supplier-related cost factors and costs in connection with global sourcing should be surveyed individually. The following cost factors should be determined and analyzed:

1. Supplier-related costs
– Direct product costs
  • Manufacturing costs
  • Development costs
  • Packaging costs
  • Freight costs (airfreight, sea freight, rail freight, truck freight)
  • Payment conditions, e. g., discount
  • Rates of duty
  • Insurance
– Indirect product costs
  • Disposal and recycling costs
  • Tool costs
  • Start of production costs
  • Repair and service costs
  • Costs for communication with the buyer's company

- Costs for guaranteeing supply, e. g., construction of a warehouse
- Costs for quality assurance
- Financing costs

The supplier-related costs listed here, as an example, are naturally not to be one-sidedly borne by the supplier. As a rule, the listed cost pools are partially to be undertaken by the buyer. It is common to attempt to transfer the costs of the intermediate warehouse on the buyer. All costs related to duty and logistics are integral components of the price composition. Here, too, the buyer should be warned. Are these costs already integrated in the product price, or are they to be paid additionally? Finally, you should try to identify all direct and indirect supplier-related costs not only to be able to calculate the actual end price per product, but also to be able to relatively quantify the price advantage of the international suppliers against the regional suppliers. As a next step, additional costs that might arise through global sourcing need to be analyzed.

2. Buyer-related costs
- Global sourcing related process costs
  - Research costs in connection with identifying products and material groups suitable for global sourcing
  - Information costs during market screening
  - Reconciliation costs while determining requirement specifications
  - Costs for searching, information costs, and communication costs in connection with international requests for proposals and the identification of suppliers
  - Initiation and agreement costs in connection with awarding the final contract of a product or material group to a supplier
  - Control and coordination costs within the framework of product dispatch and the entire global sourcing controlling

Among the buyer-related costs, that are the additional costs, the process costs that arise in connection with global sourcing are also included. A quantification of the same is possible, albeit not always helpful. For example, how do you want to account for the research costs that arise from market screening with the experience that your organization has built up through global sourcing? Many costs, naturally, can be analyzed, quantified, and offset. Do not, however, use these as arguments against global sourcing. Rather, give your company the necessary time to get acquainted with global sourcing. By doing so, the savings made through global sourcing will very quickly compensate the arising process costs and even, perhaps, clearly exceed them.

With the knowledge of product value and material group analysis, and after considering the total cost of ownership, a company is equipped with a sure basis that will help meet a global sourcing decision. However what data is necessary to conduct a product value analysis, a material group analysis, and total cost of ownership? Experts recommend conducting a three-tier process for collecting the necessary data and analyzing it.

- *Step 1:* Review the available data pool.
- *Step 2:* Complete the data pool. Only updated databases give meaningful evaluations. Important for a global sourcing decision: Check whether the available specifications are detailed enough and that they are, at the very least, in English.
- *Step 3:* Evaluate the data pool. For example, the analyses of order quantity and order value, analysis of supply conditions, and analysis of contracts on the basis of period of validity and conditions. An interesting potential for standardization can often be discovered from the evaluation.

The following data should be available to you:

Market analysis (national and international)
- Market and sector reports

Master data
- Suppliers' master data
- Material master data
- Price and discount master data

Specifications and samples

Data from financial accounts
- Account allocation data
- Creditor data

Data from materials management
- Data gathered from the merchandise information system
- Order data
- Collected and evaluated creditor data
- Quantitatively collected procurement volumes
- Analysis of demand requirements
- Invoice analysis
- Previous orders
- Past prices and conditions
- Distribution of procurement volumes to suppliers, the so-called ABC analysis
- Distribution of procurement volumes to material groups

Internal data structure
- Table of accounts
- Structure of cost centers and cost units
- Material group structure
- Classification of material (e.g., sensitive/non-sensitive, pro-duction-relevant/not production-relevant)

You should also closely examine the internal processes of your purchasing organization. How is the purchasing organization built? How are the structures of the course of activity organized? Who communicates with whom? Who is involved with whom in which procurement processes, and how? How are cross-divisional functions structured to relevant technical departments? In what form does the purchasing department communicate with the areas of research and development, production, quality assurance, stock management, sales, and finance/accounts/controlling? These are just some of the questions that should be answered in the framework of the analysis. Only one who knows the current procurement situation, complete with its strengths and weaknesses, will be able to establish global sourcing as a procurement strategy in an integrated and sustainable way.

Detailed product specification — Prerequisite for comparable offers

An exact written definition of the product details and requirements makes it possible to start a successful search for suitable suppliers and to arrive at comparable offers. This is applicable for global sourcing much more than for local sourcing. In Western countries, companies can assume that possible suppliers are not only aware of the necessary norms, but that they also abide by them.

Some readers might object that, while looking for reliable foreign suppliers, one should, at least in the initial phase, hold one's cards close to the chest, in order to stop product piracy right at the very outset. They therefore believe that giving away exact data harms more than it benefits. These fears are only partially justified and often, in fact, can be eliminated, or at least reduced to a minimum risk. Often it is enough to just minimally change the dimensions of the desired product, to create a product with a slightly different appearance. Besides, it is advisable not to request for proposal of an entire material group right away and thus allow possible inferences on the product. It is enough to inquire about very few products at the first approach and nevertheless get significant information. The fear of ideas getting stolen while making inquiries in India, Eastern Europe, and Turkey is however, unjustified.

You should give the following information about the products to potential foreign suppliers:

1. Article description
2. Number of pieces/quantity
3. Period of requirement
4. Number of requests for delivery
5. Technical data (e. g., length, height, width)
6. Material requirements

7. Permitted tolerances
8. Technical drawings (preferably as 3-D data)
9. Product illustration
10. Product sample
11. International norms/certifications (The DIN norms are not enough. In case of foodstuff, the supplier should possess international certification.)
12. Requirements of shelf life
    - for the product
    - for the tool
13. Type of packaging (e.g., europallet)
14. Packaging unit
15. Environmental requirements (e.g., return of the packaging, recycling, reprocessing)
16. Warranties
17. Logistical requirements

Formulate the profile of requirements in English when making an inquiry to hitherto unknown suppliers in India, Eastern Europe, and Turkey. The same also applies for drawings. Those wishing to source in China should employ an experienced translator and have the product specifications translated into Chinese. Not all companies in China have satisfactory knowledge of English. It should also be considered that an inquiry formulated in English or Chinese would have to be replied in the respective language.

Which country is suitable for which products

In all of the described sourcing countries, companies bear labor costs and ancillary labor costs much lower than in the Western world. It sounds almost unbelievable that a Chinese production worker earns only about 10 euro cents per hour and still delivers very good output. A similar worker in Western Europe, on the other hand, earns on an average close to 150 to 200 times that amount, that is, between 15 and 20 euros per hour. In India, a production worker earns about 47 euro cents while in Poland he earns 2.9 euros. This enormous difference looks extremely attractive at first glance. It should however not be the only deciding criterion. No company would like to procure at an affordable price but get goods of a low quality in return. The requirements of a product procured abroad are, as a rule, essentially more complex. It should, naturally, fulfill the same quality criteria as in the sourcing country, or it should be available even on short notice. These are requirements that suppliers from not all low-wage countries can fulfill to the complete satisfaction of their customers. The company head should therefore decide which country is capable of offering him the most efficient combination of low labor and material costs, while meeting all his other requirements.

Nevertheless it is advised against relocating the entire procurement to just one country for a long period of time. Instead, it is recommended to also look for efficient and reliable suppliers in some second attractive region once initial experiences in global sourcing have been gathered. This will avoid dependence on the suppliers and reduce risks through political changes, strikes, or natural catastrophes to a minimum.

It has been a long time since a country has managed to hold on to its position as the procurement paradise in a particular sector. One example in Turkey a few years ago, textiles at unrivalled prices were manufactured. Today, the Chinese textile industry has toppled the Turks from the top, over the manufacture of less demanding goods from Hungary. Turkish industry is now keenly concentrating on other areas, a typical trend that can also be seen in other branches in Western Europe. The manufacture of simple parts was, for example, relocated from Great Britain, Germany or France to Hungary not too many years ago. Today, the country supplies complex technology and manufactures successful series of models for Western car manufacturers. Companies in the erstwhile Soviet Union or Romania have now taken over the manufacture of less demanding goods from Hungary.

China, India, Turkey, and the Eastern European countries are currently the most interesting countries for efficient global sourcing. Regions in these countries receive state support in a focused manner. This is how regional competence centers arise for entire sectors. If you inform yourself about these regions, the access to product specialists in global sourcing will be enormously simplified. The

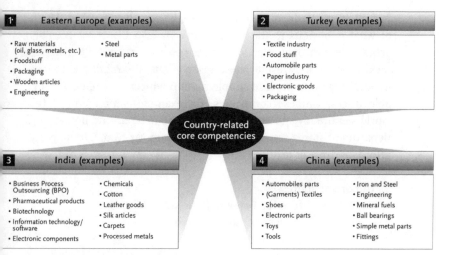

Fig. 6 Country-related core competencies
Source: Kerkhoff Consulting

competencies of companies in the countries, the technological set-up, and the qualification of the employees, however vary greatly. Figure 6 gives a first overview of what products can be procured at particularly favorable prices and in the desired quality, in which important sourcing markets worldwide.

It is advised not to look at this division as a strict guideline and rely exclusively on one region or country. Product competencies should, time and again, be put to the test. A food manufacturer, for example, had relied for decades on his agents in the Pacific region for the supply of tropical fruits. This company was surprised when it was presented with alternative suppliers from Africa and South America that could meet its annual requirements of tropical fruits at a distinctly lower price.

China: Ideal for simple mass products

Chinese industry is doing all it can to reach European levels as quickly as possible. However, most companies are still far from this goal. Therefore those who expect to get products of the highest quality will, particularly in the initial phase, be very disappointed. Much of what is obvious in the West is unknown in China, or possibly achievable, but only after long, time-consuming, and often nerve-racking attempts. Despite these reservations, the market is indeed an ideal region to procure simple mass products at extremely favorable prices. Chinese companies, for example, supply almost the world's entire toy and household appliance market. And no chain of department stores can make do without imports from China in the affordable area of textiles.

Important addresses:
- German Office for Foreign Trade, www.bfai.com
- German Chamber of Commerce in China,
  www.ahk.de/eng/index.html
- German Center for Industry and Trade,
  www.germancentre.org.cn/english/index–engl.htm
- The Government portal of PRC, www.english.gov.cn
- Ministry of Commerce of PRC, www.english.mofcom.gov.cn
- China's leading e-commerce company, www.alibaba.com
- A global source website, www.made-in-china.com
- A global source website, www.globalsources.com
- Chinese export commodities fair online,
  www.cecf.com.cn/en/index.do
- China textile network, www.chinatexnet.com
- China business, www.cityweekend.com.cn/en/beijing/cib
- China Supply Chain Council, www.supplychain.cn
- China economic review, www.chinaeconomicreview.com
- Bizshanghai online, www.bizshanghai.com.cn/project
- British chamber of commerce in shanghai,
  www.sha.britcham.org
- China trade newspaper,
  www.chinatradenews.com.cn/newse/english.asp
- Cn-Eu online-e-business platform, www.en.tops100.org

How is regional economic policy made in China? – An example from the region of Guangdong

It is true that the province on the South China Sea is not so much at the center of interest as is the economic metropolis Shanghai, which is preparing to outrank other cities in the world. Neverthe-less, Guangdong is one of the richest and most prosperous regions in China Cities like the capital, Guangzhou, or Shenzen are among the most attractive economic regions. Other cities like Shantou or Zhuhai are developing dynamically.

The reason for this positive trend lies in the fact that market economic structures were tried out in Guangdong, much before in any other province. Today, it is one of the regions that have seen the most success in the area of social market economy. Such general conditions, naturally, have an impact on the interest of potential investors and significantly shape the picture of the economy. This is how the number of privately run companies in Guangdong is way above the number in other provinces.

Small-scale industry is present in this region in the south of the People's Republic. Among the most important products here are textiles, construction materials, foodstuff, electronics, and house-hold appliances. The automobile industry is currently registering a particularly high growth rate. The broad performance portfolio also has an impact on international trade: nowhere else in China is the export and import trade as prevalent as it is here. The United States and Europe are among the most important buyers.

The course is set for further growth. The road network is ex-cellent, in fact, better than in any other region in the country. Tele-communications, almost throughout the region, is comparable to the highest international standards.

India: High-tech products and highly qualified services

India, meanwhile, is easily one of the most innovative and effi-cient countries in the areas of information technology, pharmacy, and biotechnology. In the area of BPO, India enjoys an undisputed position at the top and is intensively working on further building up this leading role. Personnel resources for further growth and high innovative power are satisfactorily present. Indian engineers and technicians are excellently qualified and match their European counterparts in every way.

Important addresses:
- German Office for Foreign Trade, www.bfai.com
- Indo-German Chamber of Commerce, www.indo-german.com
- National Association for Software and Service Companies, www.nasscom.org

How is regional economic policy made in India? – An example of Bangalore

With a population of approximately 4.6 million, Bangalore, in the Indian state of Karnataka, is one of the largest cities in India – after Mumbai, Kolkatta and Delhi. It is not just the Indian aerospace industry that is established in Bangalore. Increasingly, many national and international companies are setting up their headquarters or branch offices in this city. With its rapid development to becoming the IT-stronghold of the country, Bangalore has even earned the sobriquet »India's Silicon Valley«.

The list of international companies is only increasing. The big names in the high-tech and IT sector are already present in Bangalore and have established themselves in one of the sprawling industrial parks. Some of these companies are SAP, Motorola, IBM, Microsoft and Siemens. The prospects of finding highly qualified personnel are excellent. In this city, also called »garden city« because of its many parks, there is a satisfactory pool of first-class IT experts, willing to offer their services at absolutely justifiable rates.

Just as qualified as the IT experts are the employees of other IT-related areas. Since 2004, in this south Indian city the international news agency Reuters, in fact, collects and processes international company data for its subscribers.

Biotechnology, too, has developed into a supporting pillar of the sustainable economic boom in this city. Close to half of all Indian companies in this area are located in Bangalore.

The positive development however, does not reflect in the infrastructure. The road network is in a deplorable state. Public transport within the city is largely restricted to completely overcrowded buses. The airport is much too small, although there are plans of reconstructing it in the near future. There are, indeed, many demands yet to be met.

Turkey: Good potential for complex mass products

Turkey has, in the last few years, continuously grown from being a supplier of rummage goods to becoming a specialist for higher value goods that are mass-produced. The times are long gone when only cheap jeans were manufactured here. Today, Turkey is an attractive sourcing market for more complex products. The competence gained by the country in textile manufacture over the last few years is now used to produce fashionable garments. Italian and French designers have successfully been converting their designs into high-end garments in Turkish workshops. Turkey is already well on its way to capturing the top position in industrial textiles thus establishing itself convincingly in this dynamically developing sector. Meanwhile, intricate electronics are sourced from Turkish suppliers. The same applies for elaborate packaging.

Important addresses:
- German Office for Foreign Trade, www.bfai.com
- Turkish-German Chamber of Commerce and Industry, www.dtr-ihk.de
- Yellow pages of Turkish- German cooperation, www.ankara.diplo.de/de/03/Gelbe_Seiten/gelbe_seiten.html
- Turkey Industry Guide, www.sektorum.com/eng/
- Foreign Economic Relations Board, www.deik.org

How is regional economic policy made in Turkey? Istanbul as an example

The former Constantinople, today has a population of almost 10 million and is the economic center of Turkey. The handicrafts business and industrial firms concentrate on the production of textiles and foodstuff. Furthermore, Istanbul is also an interesting sourcing market for leather goods and ceramics. The region is fast developing in the area of technology as well. A good example for this positive trend is the growth in the manufacture of diesel motors, buses, and tractors. The increasing economic strength is also reflected in enormous construction activity. New company headquarters and elaborate office buildings are mushrooming all over the place.

A well-extended autobahn network, the country's most important port that was only recently speedily extended, and two airports take care to see that this expansive economic region is well connected.

Eastern Europe: High product competency

The automobile industry has discovered Eastern Europe as a sourcing market and production location. Fiat, heavily depending on its home market, has exploited its existing ties with Central and Eastern Europe to attempt to reverse its sliding position in Europe. To Fiat, Central and Eastern Europe serves as a cheap labor base, which may help it overcome the consequences of the integration of the European (car) market and the gradual elimination of the Japanese Voluntary Export Restraints.

Fiat has particularly built up a strong position in Poland. It produces around half of the total domestic production and has a 50% local market share. A large part of production output is exported back to Western Europe. In fact, Fiat even sought Polish government backing for a more far-reaching plan to modernise the entire Polish car industry. Fiat Poland produces, along with factories in Brazil, Turkey, India and Morocco, the Palio. The »world car« programme is Fiat's plan to reduce its dependence on car production in Italy.

With the European Community's financial support of the Eastern European EU accession countries as well as with the new commitment to adapt to international competition, the qualifications of the employees and the technical set-up required for production are consistently improving. For example, today Eastern European printing plants are often in a position to provide quality comparable to their Western counterparts, at a 40% to 50% lower price. The transfer of necessary data is carried out through the Internet. Well-established partnerships with forwarding agents ensure that the products reach the buyer within the shortest possible time.

Companies from this region are increasingly becoming important partners for Western companies that are looking at generating profits from global sourcing and that rely on short delivery times.

Further information on the most important Eastern European countries can be found under:

- German Office for Foreign Trade, www.bfai.com
- Polish-German Chamber of Commerce and Industry, www.ihk.pl
- Poland Portal, www.poland.gov.pl
- Czech-German Chamber of Commerce and Industry, www.dtihk.cz
- Portal Czech Republic Online, www.tschechien-online.org
- German-Hungarian Chamber of Commerce and Industry, www.duihk.hu
- Foreign Trade Promotion Center, www.aneir-cpce.ro
- Hungarian Investment and Trade Development Agency, www.itd.hu
- Investment and Business Development Agency, www.czechinvest.org

How is regional economic policy made in Hungary? – An example of Györ

Györ, the city in West Pannonia, the »small Hungarian low-lands«, was built in 1271. A respectable textile and engineering industry developed here in the 19th century and is even today among the growth drivers of the region. The city's strategic location in the center of the triangle comprising Vienna, Austria, Budapest, and Bratislava has given an additional thrust to the economic development of the city and its almost 130,000 inhabitants. Three universities enjoy high recognition and prepare a highly qualified next generation.

The graduates are in great demand, since the region is experiencing a continuous and dynamic boom. The international automobile and automobile spare parts industries, in particular, have discovered Györ as an ideal production location with well-qualified employees – and all this at very favorable prices. Meanwhile, it is an open secret that in these two sectors there is no grave difference between German employees and their Hungarian counterparts in terms of qualification – it is only the wages that are seas apart.

Audi is one of the companies that is benefiting from the advantages of the location. It is not just the sporty Audi TT that is manufactured in the Hungarian city. Since quite some years now, the final assembly of the A3 is also taking place in Györ. Additionally, the company, with its headquarters in the Bavarian city of Ingolstadt, Germany, also manufactures almost all its motors for the entire range of Audi cars in this city. The Norwegian concern, Norsk Hydro, manufactures cylinder heads and motor blocks at this coveted location. And these are just two examples of international automobile and automobile spare parts manufacturers who are profiting from the framework of conditions in Györ.

Sourcing market research – The first step towards finding an optimal supplier

Actually, it could all be very simple. One meets a representative of an international supplier at a trade fair, he offers an attractive price, and the stage is set for entering the world of global sourcing and, thus, for tapping new profit sources. This would truly not be too bad. In practice, however, such a process does not work. A supplier's sweet words, appealing brochures, and a bit of rudimentary information about the political and economic situation of a new sourcing market are by no means a satisfactory basis for a long-term relationship with the supplier. No potential supplier will voluntarily tell you that the employees in his country might be lacking in qualifications, or that the threat of political unrest looms large over his country, or that the particular sector is in an economically precarious situation because of lack of raw material supplies. This means that you need to take the initiative and actively conduct some strategic sourcing market research.

The stress here is on the word *active*. This is because many companies look at sourcing market research as a cumbersome, secondary task that can be confidently dispensed with once one has got to know one or the other supplier fleetingly. Others misinterpret the term *market research*. *Gablers Wirtschafts-Lexikon* (Gablers Business Lexicon) exactly defines market research as »the systematically conducted research of a specific sub-section of the market ... while consulting, above all, external sources of information.« This applies essentially just as much to the analysis of a sourcing market. Even here, it is about making the market transparent, determining the market volume of the respective sector in the country, the price development of the product to be procured, and the number of suppliers present, and getting a feel of the potential of these suppliers. Various procurement activities are then correspondingly planned, based on the information gathered, or a company simply strikes out the country from the list of potential procurement regions. With this kind of strategic sourcing market research, existing risks can be minimized and cost and supply structures can be optimized for the long term.

It is not enough to create transparency only in the initial phase. Sourcing market research is a continuous process which should accompany international sourcing activities even in the future, because it is especially in global procurement that existing situations often change very quickly. A once comparatively stable developing country, for example, could very quickly turn into a political burning point, or a region that has decided to work intensively with foreign customers in the future. Besides, it is absolutely possible that a sourcing market changes in the course of time and establishes itself as an attractive sourcing market in a completely different sector (see example of Turkey).

What differentiates international from national sourcing market research?

Those who have been conducting sourcing market research only locally until now should prepare themselves for spending more time and incurring additional expenses in order to identify and assess the structures of international markets. This can be partly justified by the fact that, although reliable current data on the political, economic, and cultural development of a country often is available, a comparison with previous years is not possible, either due to the information being insufficient, or totally absent. Another reason is that product-related market research is still in the initial phases in many regions. Sector organizations, if at all present, are in their teething years. Equally sketchy and imprecise is the collection of data about the economic sectors. It is, therefore, important to show self-initiative. One should also consider that the databases, which, as a rule, vary from country to country, make it necessary to work with specific methods of research in the regions.

This makes it inefficient from a business perspective, to conduct sourcing market research for all products that will possibly be sourced from abroad. This is why it is advisable for those beginning with global sourcing to first restrict themselves to articles with a large procurement volume, the international procurement of which could have an especially positive impact on the profit development.

The most important success factors of sourcing market research

A really significant global sourcing market research should be aimed at identifying interesting suppliers including primary and secondary collection of information. The concluding evaluation of the collected data gives rise to a so-called supplier pool. Thus the decision maker knows how many potential suppliers are available. At the same time, he can paint a picture of how the economic and political situation will develop.

The international sourcing market research fundamentally consists of a multi-tier process. Primary and secondary sourcing market research are different from each other, particularly with regard to the intensity of costs and time. Whereas the latter is mainly about profound research and assessment of existing accessible sources, primary collection of data is always about personally talking with the people concerned. Thus, the use of primary sources is more time-consuming and expensive than secondary sourcing market research. As a first step it is advisable to carry out secondary sourcing market research. This gives the buyer a first impression and an overview. The analyzed content and results of the secondary research can then in the second phase that is, primary market research, be examined in a more target-oriented manner. You could use the secondary research as a first filter of the sourcing requirements and closely examine the knowledge thus gathered through precise interviews in the framework of primary sourcing market research.

Primary sourcing market research	Secondary sourcing market research
Generation of information from: • Visits to trade fairs • Visits to companies • Talks with experts and suppliers • Talks with banks, forwarding agents, Chambers of Commerce, etc. • Business trips to the sourcing markets • Seminars and trade conventions • etc.	Generation of information from: • Trade fair catalogs • Foreign trade information • Trade journals and articles • Chambers of Commerce and Industry • Online databanks • Supplier lists • Trade associations (BME, VDI, etc.) • Banks and thrift institutions • etc.

... leads to the supplier pool

Fig. 7 International sourcing market research
Source: Kerkhoff Consulting

Often, it is asked, what exactly should be analyzed? It is not, in fact, about describing a supplier, or his ability related to the product or service, in detail. This is possible only after identifying the potential suppliers. More important is the description of supplier markets, legalities in the sectors, and other market peculiarities. Typical questions that should be answered systematically within the framework of international sourcing market research are:

- Which peculiarities of the region/country should be considered?
- Which suppliers offer the product or service to be procured, and at what price?
- How large is the relevant supplier market (volume)?
- How the relevant supplier market is structured, that is, which price-quality segments exist there?
- Which specialized quality assurance companies are there in the supplier market under consideration? Which logistics experts or other external service providers exist?
- How attractive are the individual segments?
- How will the relevant supplier market develop in the next three to five years?
- What does the value chain look like in the market under consideration?

- What connections exist in the value chain to preliminary and downstream companies? Are there any dependencies?
- Which typical trends are to be expected in the future in the relevant supplier market under consideration?
- What are the current price levels of the offered products or services in the relevant supplier market? How have these developed in the last five years?
- Who is the typical customer of the supplying company? How long has the supplying company already been working together with its customers?
- How can entry barriers into the supplier market be described?
- Which dependencies exist between supplier and customers?
- Which success factors are to be fulfilled at which level?
- Which legalities exist between supplier market and sales market?
- How can the role of the suppliers of the supplying company be described?
- How international is the supply market today, how was it five years ago, how will it be five years from now?
- How many relevant suppliers are there in which region?
- What is the market share of the supplying companies?
- On the basis of which criteria can the supplying companies be described (size, employees, turnover, regional coverage, experience in years, etc.)?
- How can the various supplying companies be assessed? What are their strengths and weaknesses? What opportunities and threats exist from the point of view of the procuring company?
- Are there new materials that can substitute the existing product offers?
- Are there completely new supplying companies entering the market?
- What are your direct competitors doing differently in connection with the supplying companies?

How can questions of the type listed above, as an example, be systematically answered? Which sources can be tapped? To explain the same, a practical example is presented. It is about a company that, in the past, was procuring from three wholesalers and was, therefore, completely convinced of getting excellent prices. With the idea of avoiding the dealers and communicating directly with the suppliers abroad, the consultant met with a complete lack of understanding. Finally, he could, indeed, convince his client with the help of the possible cost-cutting potential. This is not an isolated case. The dread of ceasing longstanding business relations is in many industries still immense. In the course of globalization, however, completely new suppliers are emerging. Old legalities do not apply any more. The following information will help the timely identification of the new rules of the game.

Sources of secondary sourcing market research

The complexities of many sourcing markets and of the products that possibly will be sourced require the assessment of many sources to receive the necessary differentiated information. Experience, however continues to show that companies take the easy way out with the generation of data and merely restrict themselves to using databanks or institutions in their home countries or in the respective country. This does, indeed, give them a certain basic knowledge. Assessments of various transnational organizations such as the World Bank, the EU, or the OECD, however, help in reaching more precise and focused decisions related to the comparison of various markets. Access to these facts is also no more complex than procuring information from other institutions. Often, all that is required is the click of a mouse, and the path to getting help with this decision is free – through the Internet. It is important to pay heed to how old the facts are. Particularly in developing countries the situation changes very quickly. You could also make use of the supplier databanks. Among these, for example, are www.china suppliers.com for China, www.exportersindia.com for India, www. turkfreezone.com for Turkey, www.abc.cz for Czech Republic, www. polishbusiness.net for Poland and worldwide search engines like www.kompass.com or www.globalsources.com.

A multitude of organizations, associations and authorities have comprehensive material that you could use for your global sourcing market research. These pages are mostly available free of cost on the Internet.

A selection of renowned aids for all those, who wish to give a new thrust to their company profits through global sourcing:

- German Chambers of Commerce Abroad, www.ahk.de/eng/index.html
- Federal Foreign Office, www.auswaertiges-amt.com/www/en/index_html
- Associations of banks and thrift institutions
- Sector-specific associations, e. g., German Engineering Federation, www.vdma.org/wps/portal/Home/en
- German Office for Foreign Trade, www.bfai.com
- China suppliers, www.chinasuppliers.alibaba.com
- Credit reform, www.creditreform.de
- Council of German Chambers of Commerce – DIHT, www.diht.de
- European Union – EU, www.europa.eu.int/index–en.htm
- Exporters India, www.exportersindia.com
- Trade associations, e. g., German Materials Management, Procurement, and Logistics Association – BME, www.bme.de
- Sector-specific trade journals
- Global Sources; search engine for products and suppliers from all over the world, www.globalsources.com
- Sourcing Asia, Asian trade journal
- China Contract, Chinese newsletter
- Hamburg Institute of International Economics, www.hwwa.de/hwwa–engl.html
- Trade representations of the sourcing regions in Germany or in other countries
- Institute for Economic Research – Ifo, www.ifo.de
- Kompass; information about national and international products and services, www.kompass.com
- Supplier databanks for the respective countries
- Trade fair catalogues
- Organization for Economic Cooperation and Development OECD, www.oecd.org
- TurkFreeZone, www.turkfreezone.com/english/index.asp
- United Nations – UN, www.un.org
- World Bank, www.worldbank.org

- Wer liefert was?; search engine for products and services of European companies, www.wlw.de/start/DE/en/index.html
- www.infobroker.de; search engine for identifying suppliers and conducting market analyses, www.infobroker.de/indexe. html
- Alibaba, China, www.alibaba.com
- Global Sources, Hong Kong, www.globalsources.com
- EC21, Korea, www.ec21.com
- EC Plaza, Korea, www.ecplaza.com
- AsianNet, Asia, www.asianet.com
- Commerce Online, Taiwan, www.commerce.com.tw
- Transworld Trade Net, Taiwan, www.ttnet.net
- Taiwan Trade, www.taiwantrade.com.tw
- Asian Products, Taiwan, www.asianproducts.com
- Busy Trade, Hong Kong, www.busytrade.com

Sources of primary sourcing market research

In primary sourcing market research the companies rely on themselves becoming active and gaining a personal impression. This is what makes the primary acquisition of information the most expensive and time-consuming part of the necessary market research. Even if the budget for tapping new sourcing regions is lean, no company that wishes to profit in the long term from the benefits of global sourcing should dispense with such activities.

These measures offer the necessary aid in reaching a decision:

- *Visits to trade fairs:* There is probably no other event that is more conducive to making contact with the relevant people than at an international trade fair. These fairs are exclusively attended by companies that have already gathered experience in exports, or that have decided to capture Western countries with their products. At trade fairs, it is not just the offers that can be compared to one another. The various presentations, too, give important information, about how professionally or unprofessionally the exhibitors act while canvassing for customers. Every so often, this helps one infer, whether the exhibitor is already in a position to cater to the needs of global customers. Often, however, delegates from other companies also attend the stalls at the trade fairs. They might be playing with the idea of sourcing globally, or might even already be procuring from foreign suppliers for a long time. Often, it is a great help talking to them, and asking them about their experiences with global sourcing and with working with a particular supplier. It is, however, advisable not to evaluate the presence of a potential supplier at a trade fair too highly. The Association of the German Trade Fair Industry (AUMA), www.auma.de, keeps ready information about international trade fairs. Similarly, every country has a local organization that regularly updates information about international trade fairs. You could profit from the trade fair even if you do not have the time to actually attend it; exhibition catalogs help. Those interested can find all participating companies with their main areas of focus featured in the catalogs. One can then approach them.

- *Visits to companies:* On the very first orientation trip to a new sourcing market, you are not supposed to conduct detailed negotiations. It would be too early at this stage, where one has too little information about the competitors and the general conditions in the respective country. This trip is all about gaining a first impression. For example, how is the technical set-up of the business? Are modern production processes employed? How is the infrastructure at the company headquarters? Are there possibly any incentives from the state for foreign investors? These are only a handful of questions to which answers should be found right on the very first trip, in order to support the decision-making process. Such a trip should, naturally, be meticulously planned, since an important decision of the company depends on the results of this trip. The Chambers of Commerce Abroad of the respective country, representative offices of some sectors, as well as representative offices of the sourcing markets in the home country help with the preparation. Often, common trips for the sector are organized.
- *Talks with colleagues from the sector, suppliers, competitors, logistics companies, and so on:* Future-oriented owners of companies and their employees at managerial positions are increasingly

aware of the high value of an efficient procurement management. Often, this is why they no longer shy away from discussing their procurement methods with colleagues from the sector, as they did in the past. In many cases, this exchange of experiences helps both sides. It is, therefore, advisable not to dispense with doing the same. Likewise, suppliers should be included in the global sourcing market research. On the one hand, it will, as a rule, have a positive impact on how accommodating they are at upcoming negotiations, when they are informed that a customer is at least playing with the idea of procuring abroad. On the other hand, larger suppliers, above all, know the international competition very well. One should not dispense with this information, even when it can, in some cases, turn out to be not entirely objective.

- *Talks with banks and thrift institutions:* Credit institutes like to hear that their clients are making use of modern procurement methods and, by doing so, want to improve their profit situation. This is why such activities are assigned plus points in ratings. With their international networks, banks can, often, even help with concrete information during global sourcing market research.
- *Talks with Chambers of Commerce:* The Chambers of Commerce make efforts to help their members. When it is about making contacts in international markets, the large Chambers, in particular, offer effective support, because of their cross-border cooperation. It is, indeed, worthwhile to make an inquiry.
- *Talks with forwarding agents:* It is not just the international forwarding agents that benefit from global sourcing. Smaller transport companies, too, are discovering the new form of procurement as a lucrative business. These service providers, therefore, not only know the transport tariffs; they are also very well informed about the necessary formalities in the supplier's country and in the home market, rates of duty, and the import conditions. This information is very important for companies beginning with global sourcing, because it does occasionally come about that the cost savings as a result of lower labor and material costs, are totally sapped by transportation costs and duties.

– *Visits to seminars and trade conventions:* The topic global sourcing is increasingly taking up more space in the event catalogs of institutes for further education. The qualifications of the speakers and the imparted know-how, however, frequently do not correspond to the requirements of the complex topic. Take care to see, therefore, that the trainer has a well-founded experience in international procurement and does not merely have theoretical knowledge. If the aim of the seminar is to impart information on an expansive sourcing market, then the following points should be handled in the seminar: (1) products and services that can be procured internationally, (2) supplier-related research, (3) international request for proposal, (4) supply and payment conditions, (5) visits to suppliers and selection of suppliers, (6) quality management, and (7) contracts and agreements. The essential political, demographic, and economic benchmark figures and the latest data on trade between the two countries should also be presented. At trade conventions, too, the speakers should, likewise, possess the necessary practical knowledge and not be restricted to theoretical information. It is good if entrepreneurs from the respective country are also sitting on the podium.

Once one or more potential sourcing markets have been analyzed, it is important to clearly process the information generated from the primary and secondary sources, and to carefully evaluate them. Allot some space in the schemata prepared by you, so that you can regularly update the evaluations. By doing so, on the one hand, you take it as your duty to consistently conduct sourcing market research, and, on the other hand, you will always have significant data at your disposal that could bring in plus points even during talks with a bank. After all, as mentioned earlier, credit institutes have high regard for corporate clients who work intensively with efficient methods of procurement.

The most common mistakes made during sourcing market research

Market research is time-consuming and expensive – especially, when the market that needs to be studied has been largely unexploited. But it is worth it. Many companies take liberties with the analysis of a potential sourcing market, and are, therefore, very disappointed with their decision for a particular sourcing market and the suppliers located there. Those who make sourcing market research a fundamental element of global sourcing, however, do not need to worry too much about whether their activities will be successful.

The mistakes made during sourcing market research are, as a rule, always the same. Therefore, we present here the gravest mistakes, so that similar mistakes will not be made in practice:

- Companies select the first supplier that comes along.
- Companies do not look for additional potential suppliers.
- Companies think that merely getting to know each other for the first time at a trade fair or a similar occasion is enough to start doing business together.
- One relies on the information of the suppliers, without comparing the information with what is readily available through the secondary sources.
- Reference customers of the supplier in Western countries are not contacted.

Thus, very often, one operates on blind faith, or the management or the employees authorized on their behalf sometimes do not have enough motivation to find the necessary information. Merely identifying a supplier who makes an interesting price offer at the first instance is not enough. Sustainable profitable global sourcing demands a readiness to think and act strategically, that is, in a future-oriented manner.

From supplier information to Best-in-Class supplier for global sourcing

An important advantage of global sourcing is in many cases, the enormous cost-cutting potential. Whether such potential can actually be developed or not, depends on the comparability of international and national offers. It is absolutely possible that the quotation of the price offered by a foreign supplier may sound very interesting at first, but on looking closely may not be so attractive any more. The reason could be, for example, that the offer in comparison with other offers deviates in quality, dimensions, warranty, or delivery dates. Such divergences, however, cannot be justified by thinking that the supplier does not give quality the top priority. Very often, the reason is inadequately and sketchily formulated requests for proposals that do not give the receiver any detailed specifications for formulating the offer.

It would, naturally, be too time-consuming to send detailed requests for proposals to all suppliers who have been identified during the sourcing market research, and who could be in a position to supply the desired products. A multi-tier selection process is recommended to separate the wheat from the chaff. The figure shows the ideal approach for identifying the Best-in-Class supplier:

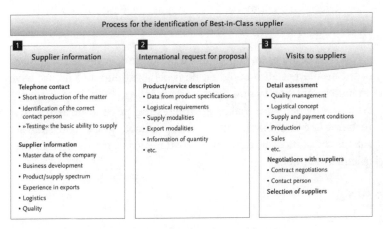

Fig. 8 Process for the identification of Best-in-Class supplier
Source: Kerkhoff Consulting

Supplier information

As a first step, one should gather initial details about the production program, manufacturing processes and previous success in exports of all companies that have been included in the supplier pool. Often a mere telephone call suffices, though this too should be carefully prepared, of course. Therefore, while preparing it is necessary to determine the exact contact details and to identify the people responsible for sales. Language problems can significantly influence the success of the talks. Therefore, it makes sense that the first telephone contact is made by employees or agents who are fluent in the language of the respective country. This especially holds true when researching Chinese companies and small and medium-sized companies in other sourcing markets. Those who speak fluent English, though, can be assured of finding competent contact persons in India and Eastern Europe. Occasionally, even German or French is understood. Even if it might seem unimaginable for a Westerner as the infrastructural prerequisites in many regions are far from what we have reached here in Europe. One should therefore, be prepared for bad telephone lines and unavailable Internet connections. Nevertheless, a potential »global sourcer« does not avoid such preliminary talks, if he wishes to filter out the very best suppliers from his supplier pool. Make a particularly impressive portrayal of your company. Name your main areas of focus and your strengths and give the potential supplier a picture of the advantages that could arise out of such business cooperation. Through adept questioning, try to gain sensitive information like amount and development of turnover, or market share. The supplier pool can be reduced further after the telephone inquiries.

Suppliers who were convincing during the telephone inquiries receive a form in which their information is to be filled in and sent back to the company. In this phase, it is all about adding to the information gained during the first contact and generating additional data that will help in the final selection of the supplier. It should not necessarily be interpreted as disinterest, if a company, to whom you have sent a form, does not send you the required information within a few days. Many companies are unaccustomed to such inquiries, which is why they do not attribute much importance to them. It is worthwhile, therefore, to call up the company and remind them to send in the form; otherwise an important contact could be lost.

The supplier information should contain the following points:

1. *Master data of the company*
   - full description, including trading name of the company and year of establishment
   - address, telephone, fax, e-mail, homepage, contact person, and function
   - locations within the country and abroad (development, manufacture, sales)
   - private or state-run companies

2. *Business development*
   - group to which company belongs, size of business, areas of operation
   - economic development in the last three years (turnover, profit)
   - turnover in every area of operation
   - number of employees in every area of operation

3. *Spectrum of products and services*
   - product range
   - capacities
   - additional services (e. g., development)

4. *Experience in exports*
   - number of years
   - export regions
   - share of exports in the total turnover
   - European references (companies, contact persons with contact details, duration of business relations)

5. *Logistics*
   - warehouse (e. g., location, capacity, set-up)
   - consignment stock
   - supply conditions

6. *Quality management*
- available quality management
- name of the company checking quality

After the suppliers return the forms filled in with their information, the company needs to evaluate the same. Traditional key figures like size of the company, number of employees, turnover and capacities can be used for the evaluation. Besides the traditional key figures one should also check in detail the export data provided by the potential supplier. This could, for example, contain information about the goods that the company exports, the Western references that have been named, and the company's experience in exports. After assessing the questionnaires, the number of potential suppliers will again reduce. In this way, companies that have had a very brief experience in exports, or that had to answer the questions about available quality management or references with a clear »no«, are eliminated at the very outset. With regard to striking developments, for example, extraordinary jumps in the turnover or profit, it is recommended to have this information explained during a further telephone conversation. It is advisable to take the time to check some of the references that have been mentioned by talking to them over the telephone, or by paying them a visit. Make use of these inquiries to develop closer contact with buyers from other companies and, in this way, to build a network.

The following catalog of questions can help with these talks:
- How do the type, depth, duration, and frequency of cooperation appear?
- How high is the order volume?
- Is further cooperation planned? If no, why not?
- How are the type, classification, quality, and price level of the products?
- What storage possibilities are available?
- How do the logistics function?
- What supply and payment conditions were agreed upon?
- How are complaints handled?
- How exactly are deadlines met?
- Which external possibilities are available for quality control?

International request for proposal

After conducting the inquiries as described, prospective »global sourcers« will be in a position to further narrow down the list of potential suppliers. They will then be able to send an international request for proposal to all suppliers who have had a positive assessment in the selection process until now. These differ from the request for proposal sent out to local suppliers, in the significantly higher degree of detail. The essential points should, however, be comparable to a national request for proposal. Among these are, naturally, the characteristics of quality. In Western countries, it suffices to merely name the norm. Such standardized information, however, means very little to suppliers especially from developing countries. The only option then is to explain, in detail, the requirements that are concealed in the quality norms which absolutely need to be observed. The place of delivery should, likewise, be exactly defined, since this can have a very large impact on the expected costs. The so-called Incoterms (International Commercial Terms) too, are an important basis for calculations and should, therefore, be fixed in the request for proposal. These regulate, among other things, the form and place of delivery by the supplier. The following table explains the four most important Incoterms:

	Name	Export*	Import*	Transport contract	Place of delivery	Transfer of risks	Transfer of costs
EXW	Ex Works	Buyer	Buyer	Buyer	Supplier's place of business	Place of delivery	Place of delivery
FOB	Free on Board	Supplier	Buyer	Buyer	Ship (port of shipment)	Ship's rail	Ship's rail
CFR	Cost and Freight	Supplier	Buyer	Supplier	Ship (port of shipment)	Ship's rail	Port of destination
CIF	Cost, Insurance, Freight	Supplier	Buyer	Supplier	Ship (port of shipment)	Ship's rail	Port of destination

*Export and import clearance = Undertaking the costs of customs clearance of the exports
and procurement of the necessary documents in the country of export or import

Fig. 9 Most common international supply conditions
Source: Kerkhoff Consulting

The actual payment conditions should also be included in an international request for proposal. This is because terms that might be prevalent in the West, like cash discount for an early payment, can be totally unknown in many countries. Finally, the currency in which the delivery is to be calculated should also be laid down. A contract drawn on euro basis, for example, would restrict the currency risk caused by changes due to rising exchange rates in the sourcing country, which can otherwise impact the prices negatively. Those who pay attention to these requirements can be sure to get comparable offers and then be able to select the best supplier.

It is recommended not to send a request for proposal only to potential suppliers; forwarding agents also, too, need to know which services they should bring, such as information on the dimensions of the products, the location of the warehouse, the volume and number of requests for delivery, transportation requirements (e. g., refrigerator vehicles), as well as the estimated duration of the supply agreement. The resulting offers are comparable and create a necessary basis for reaching a decision to select the most efficient forwarding agent. Nevertheless, the buyer should obtain references for the forwarding agent, before the ultimate award of contract. After all, there are companies in every sector that do not keep to their verbal agreements.

After the response of the international request for proposal and analysis of all data, the number of suppliers in question further reduces. In Often, in connection with the international request for proposal, the supplier is also often requested to provide a product sample (sampling). Such a step is definitely recommended, if it does not prove to be too expensive and time-consuming. This will enable the technical department to make a concrete check on the product and to ascertain, whether the product meets the mark in terms of quality. Sometimes, a whole list of preliminary tests needs be conducted, before a detailed secondary test of suppliers can follow. Here, too, a sampling is recommended. Samples can also aid in refuting, at an early stage, the prejudices that exist in the technical department. It continues to be a surprise how a sample often wipes away the doubts in the minds of the technicians. Nothing could be worse than having gone well ahead with the process of global sourcing, only to fall back on sourcing within the region because the technical department could not be satisfied early on.

Normally, the circle of suppliers who should be considered seriously quickly reduces to less than ten, after the stages of collecting supplier information and making the international request for proposal. These last eight or ten suppliers should then be examined even more meticulously. Experience shows that here, too, companies tend to save at the wrong place. Visiting a supplier is quite uncommon even in the Western world. With the suppliers being located beyond the borders, the barriers against a personal visit are even higher. Therefore, one should absolutely avoid the mistake of not calling on the suppliers in question personally.

Visits to suppliers – The final decision for a foreign partner

With the earlier checks and assessment the number of potential suppliers with whom it would be beneficial to have a long-term cooperation can be narrowed down to eight to ten. That brings you to the final selection. The following main criteria are the focus of this selection:

- Quality management
- Logistics concept
- Supply and payment conditions
- International negotiating strategy

In addition, there is a host of other criteria that should be checked. Allow me to begin with the first two main fields, mentioned above that, which should be checked. It is important to take the time to check every individual point and to reach a judgment on the respective situation of the suppliers who have made it to the last round. By doing so, the basis for reaching a decision is created, and later, you can very likely be sure of having made the right decision.

In focus: Quality management

The decision to select a particular supplier should essentially depend on his likelihood to fulfill the predetermined agreements and requirements in the long term. Thus, the prerequisite that the potential supplier is able to ensure the necessary quality in a sustainable manner becomes an important criterion for the selection of the supplier. This is why one should pay particular attention to the available quality management system. It is not enough to merely rely on verbal assurances; what matters are verifiable facts.

After all a recognized and actively implemented quality management system makes sure that the supplier can achieve the following:

- guarantee customer satisfaction
- fulfill the customers' requirements based on the processes defined in the system at all times
- discover mistakes well in time and, if possible, avoid them
- regularly check and consistently improve the effectiveness and efficiency of the processes

Right from the stage of making the first contact and during the international request for proposal, the inability to follow international norms and standards will be a criterion for elimination from the supplier pool. Those who produce according to these regulations, however, prove that they are, indeed, capable of manufacturing products of the highest quality. Some of the important international norms and standards are ISO 9000 and ISO 14000. Meanwhile, more than 160,000 companies in some 160 countries follow these norms.

- *ISO 9000 standards* are objectives and organizational requirements for quality assurance systems. By observing these norms, companies can prove that their products and services are of a consistent quality.
- *ISO 14000 standards* are concerned with the areas of the environment and environmental management. By accepting these norms, companies can prove that they wish to avoid any damaging influences on the environment and wish to continuously improve their »environmental performance«.

Most companies are completely overworked when it comes to checking whether the potential new suppliers actually observe the norms and standards. The seal of approval, after all, is not enough to ensure high quality. Often enough, the norm indications are crudely falsified. Highly qualified help, however, is available. There exist renowned, independent organizations in the sourcing countries that undertake the necessary initial checks, as well as the ongoing quality checks during production. On request, these quality experts also check packaging, storage, and shipping, carry out work sampling, and supervise the loading of goods, as well as the orderly entry of quantities. In case damages arise, the organizations are, likewise, operative.

Among these neutral testing organizations are TÜV Rheinland and the SGS Group. TÜV Rheinland offers its services in 31 European and in 17 Asian countries, and is also present in North and South America, and Africa. The SGS Group has offices in 140 countries worldwide and is at the top of the list of globally active, independent quality-testing organizations. It is recommended to contact these organizations and to invite suitable offers, because in most cases, these organizations perform very good work and save their clients expensive and time-consuming quality problems. Nevertheless, you should check at regular intervals to find out whether the testing organization is actually continuing to work diligently.

In focus: Logistics concept

Logistics is one of the instruments of the strategic corporate strategy and should ensure a guaranteed supply of goods in these times of just-in-time and reducing warehouse scope. Many boards of directors or CEOs and their management teams have, however, not yet recognized this fact, and continue to neglect storage and transportation costs in their calculations. That is an unforgivable lapse, especially in the context of logistics, where various factors are to be considered, like personnel costs, capital lockup due to material stock, or allowance for depreciation.

Global sourcing sets very special, additional requirements on logistics. The issue of supply guarantee is gaining in importance because of the large distances to be spanned. Having a buffer warehouse in the country of the supplier, as well as in the vicinity of the buyer can reduce or even eliminate the risk of a stop in the production due to the delivery failing to arrive, and should, therefore, definitely be constructed. Such precautionary measures naturally cost money, and should, therefore, be considered when comparing costs between global and local sourcing. A consignment stock, from which a buyer can draw out goods based on his need and only then have to pay for them, is normally set up by a supplier only for customers who buy large volumes from him, and with whom he has already established a close business relationship. As already mentioned, it is advisable not to source the entire requirement from abroad, but to continue to have an existing supplier manufacture for a part of the products – even if the costs for the same are clearly higher.

Constructing a warehouse in a hitherto unknown sourcing market requires the know-how of a professional, because not all who own a warehouse somewhere provide the necessary service. It is not just the goods that sometimes place complex demands on the place of storage, for example, by requiring special temperatures or shelf systems. The protection against burglary, which continues to be a problem in smaller developing countries, needs to be ensured as well. To that end, the logistics experts should have a comprehensive service portfolio and an excellent reputation. The only possibility then, just as when selecting a suitable partner, is to prepare a request for proposal containing all requirements up to the last detail and to obtain references for potential companies. After the evaluation, one should check whether the expenses for the necessary logistics actually justify awarding the contract to a supplier in this sourcing market. A prospective »global sourcer« need not, however, be afraid simply due to the large distance. International transport chains are continuously being optimized and being made more flexible. The rapid development in information technology also contributes to the same.

In focus: Supply and payment conditions

Many companies still look at supply and payment conditions as a cumbersome formality that one has to engage in. Many overlook the possible negative effects of incomplete formulations. Especially in international trade, supply and payment conditions can be a deciding factor between success and failure. This is why all those who wish to derive maximum profit from sourcing abroad should carefully check the conditions demanded by the supplier.

While carrying out this check, one should duly try to fathom the possible effects on the following aspects:

- the current political and economic situation in the sourcing market
- the necessary liquidity and credit requirement
- the possibilities of financing
- the existing currency risk

To be able to conduct this assessment, one should get a general idea of the many variations of supply and payment conditions. Nevertheless, in the initial phases of a business relationship, suppliers can be argued out of their demands only with great difficulty. With the course of time, after the first few orders have been successfully carried out, the trust between the partners grows, and so does the readiness to provide concessions.

Here is an overview of the most important payment conditions for international business. They are categorized as non-documentary and documentary:

1. Non-documentary payment conditions
- *Payment on »open account« (clean payment):* The most favorable payment condition for buyers, because the supplier dispenses with any kind of guarantee of payment. In most cases, however, such accommodation is shown only in longstanding business relations.
- *Cash before delivery/advance payment:* The worst payment condition for buyers.
- *Cash down payment/installments:* Such payment conditions are normally made, if the delivery time is long. In this type of payment, the buyer and supplier at least share the risk to a certain extent.
- *Cash on delivery – COD:* This payment condition is not so flattering for the buyer, because it signalizes the low trust that the

supplier places on the buyer's payment morals. It is normally restricted to land and air transport in business abroad. The forwarding agent undertakes the collection on delivery.

2. Documentary payment conditions

– *Documents against acceptance:* Here, the supplier authorizes his credit institute to hand over the necessary documents that entitle the buyer to the goods only against payment or on acceptance of a bill of exchange. The buyer, however, has to risk making the payment before being able to check the goods. Handing over the documents can follow any of these payment conditions:

- Cash against documents – CAD or documents against payment – D/P: The documents are handed over against payment of the full purchase price.
- Documents against acceptance – D/A: The buyer is allowed time for payment, which is guaranteed by a bill of exchange.
- Letter of credit: In this case, the supplier receives the purchase price from a bank, as soon as he submits particular documents. The credit institute collects the invoice amount from the buyer or his bank, and, by doing so, also undertakes the risk of non-payment. A particular advantage of a letter of credit: The importer can be assured that the supplier receives his payment only on proving the fulfillment of all credit terms with the help of documents.

These are the types of letters of credit:

– *Irrevocable letter of credit/revocable letter of credit:* Normally, letters of credit are irrevocable, because revocable letters of credit can be changed or annulled by the issuing bank – without the consent of the exporter – up until the receipt of the documents.
– *Non-confirmed letter of credit/confirmed letter of credit:* In case of non-confirmed letters of credit, the foreign bank of the importer is exclusively liable for payment of the purchase price. In case of confirmed letters of credit, one more bank, mostly

the credit institute of the supplier, is authorized to give an additional promise to pay.

- *Sight payment/deferred payment:* In case of sight payment, there exists a concurrent exchange, that is, payment is made against the presentation of documents to the bank. The credit institute gets a maximum of seven days to check the presented documents. Deferred payment includes the time for payment.
- *Revolving letter of credit:* This type of letter of credit is agreed upon, in order to hedge receivables that are due from longer supply contracts.

Fundamentally, companies should prefer clean payment from all payment conditions. Do not, however, make the mistake of seeing payment conditions detached from the logistics concept. This could prove to be very costly. Companies also prefer the Incoterm CIF (cost, insurance, freight). This apparent »all-round worry-free package« does, indeed, assure delivery up to the port of shipment; however, there is no direct influence on the forwarding costs and the selection of the forwarding agent. Therefore, always stipulate the Incoterms Ex Works or Free on Board. With these, the selection of the logistics experts lies with the buyer, and the conditions are then directly negotiable. How does an ideal, typical process look? The figure below should help clarify:

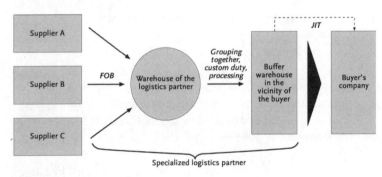

Fig. 10 Ideal logistics process
Source: Kerkhoff Consulting

The supplier supplies FOB to a warehouse or a consignment stock. Here, a logistics partner groups together goods of various suppliers and brings these goods to the destination country. He undertakes all administrative processes, as well as custom duty, and also operates a buffer warehouse in the vicinity of the factory, where the customer can access the required material. With the construction of buffer warehouses, just-in-time delivery (JIT) is also no longer a problem.

In focus: First personal impression

Once the supplier pool is reduced to a fairly small number of potential candidates, it is essential to have a look at the company before coming to a final decision. It is, of course, a known fact from daily life: The first impression, often, contributes significantly to the final decision. The costs incurred due to the visit and the time spent there are, in our experience, completely indispensable. Unless, of course, one is considering production of parts that demand very little technological and manufacturing expertise, and that can even be manufactured by modestly qualified employees. In all other cases, a visit is essential.

The following questions would, then, be part of the checklist:
- Is the material warehouse tidy and clearly sorted?
- How are the goods packed in the dispatch warehouse?
- How is the set-up in the quality control and development departments?
- How clean and modern are the production facilities, administration buildings, and outdoor facilities?
- Are the employees neatly dressed?
- Do the employees in the export department master the English language?

Therefore, with this research, it is evident that one can gather important impressions about the actual state of affairs in the workplace of a potential supplier. The old proverb, »paper does not blush«, also applies to supplier information or the participation in the requests for proposals. It is, therefore, advisable to take sufficient time for the visit and to closely observe the production processes on site. As far as possible, the employees should not notice any of this and should carry on with their work as usual in an uninhibited manner. Furthermore, try to have a look at the consignment labels of the finished goods in the dispatch warehouse. The names of the recipients not only function as additional references but also give information on competitors. It is also interesting to know whether a few competitors could, in fact, be customers of the potential supplier. Additionally, it is helpful to equip your employees with a comprehensive checklist when they visit the supplier. This catalog of questions integrates all areas of the company, which are necessary for assessing the supplier. Even when this catalog is very comprehensive, a step-by-step execution is recommended. At the end of the day, this is the only way one can assess a supplier in detail. Here is an example of a possible checklist:

Checklist: Personal supplier assessment on site
Quality management system
1. Does the supplier have a comprehensive quality management handbook?
2. Are the quality processes regularly checked?
3. Does the supplier have a detailed quality compendium/handbook for the employees?
4. Has the management formulated strategies, responsibilities, and objectives of the quality control department?
5. Are the employees well versed with the regulations and strategies presented in the quality handbook?
6. Does the company conduct quality training?
7. Does the quality manager report to the top management?
8. Are satisfactory personnel, infrastructural, and mechanical resources available, in order to achieve the quality specifications?
9. Does the management of the company regularly conduct reviews?
10. Are deviations in the quality considered during these checks, and are corresponding measures taken to eliminate such deficits?

11. Is the performance of the suppliers included in the reviews?
12. Does the management check customer satisfaction?
13. Does a further quality assurance system exist, in addition to quality control during production and upon completion?
14. Do the quality auditors have special training; do they not report to the production department?
15. Does the production department have control charts at critical locations, which give information on problems that have arisen?
16. Is the production process immediately corrected or stopped, if problems in quality surface?

Procurement management
1. Is the procurement carried out on the basis of satisfactory, written instructions?
2. Are customer requirements considered right at the stage of procurement?
3. Are suppliers systematically assessed?
4. Does the company use an approved list of suppliers during all procurement processes?
5. Is there a prescribed process to select new suppliers?
6. How high is the percentage of defective material in the procurement volume?

Stock management
1. Is the quality of the incoming goods consistently examined?
2. Do the controls ensure that no unchecked material finds its way into the stock or into the production department?
3. Does the checked material clearly indicate the positive or negative test result?
4. Is rejected material separated clearly from suitable material?

Documentation
1. Is there an efficient system for handling and archiving customer-specific documents?
2. Is the implementation of changes resting on customer wishes carefully checked?
3. Are records prepared on the quality checks?

Order processing
1. Are orders checked to ascertain whether all requirements are met during their processing?
2. Are departments like production or quality control also involved in these checks?
3. Does the company send an acknowledgement of an order with all details, for example, quantity or quality?
4. Is there a possibility of following the production status of an order right from receipt up to delivery?
5. Does a mandatory process exist to forward the necessary information to the concerned departments for checking the order?

Design and development
1. Are design specifications, including the specific wishes of the customers, clearly defined, and are these documented?
2. Is the design checked at regular intervals?
3. Is the final design compared with the requirements of the customer?
4. Are changes in the design checked and approved by authorized personnel?

Calibration
1. Are all necessary measuring instruments and devices checked at regular intervals for exactness?
2. Are the calibration standards comparable to national and international standards?
3. Is the calibration carried out by a qualified team?
4. Are rejected tools and measuring instruments disposed off?
5. Are new or processed tools calibrated before the first use?

Production and process controls
1. Does the company use an efficient system to keep a check on production processes?
2. Are there process controls, like tests, at important points in the production?
3. Are changes in production processes checked, approved, and documented?

4. Does the process control system initiate necessary measures in case problems surface?
5. Are the necessary measures documented?
6. In the recent past, have there been customer complaints due to internal process failures?

Closure check
1. Is the closure check conducted by employees who are not part of the production team?
2. Is there a satisfactory technical set-up, as well as detailed instructions for the closure check, and are these actually used?
3. Is the closure check systematically conducted for all products, or are random samples taken?
4. Does the closure check contain a check on whether customer requirements are fulfilled with regard to labeling, etc.?
5. Are the results of the closure check systematically documented?

Handling deviations in quality
1. Is there a committee that identifies the reasons for fundamental deviations in quality?
2. Does the committee include employees from all concerned departments?
3. Are the reasons for fundamental deviations in quality collectively examined?
4. Is the defective material carefully checked, separated from other material, and documented?
5. Are instructions for further handling of the material given by employees authorized to do so?
6. Is there a sectioned off zone, in which the defective material can be stored?
7. Is access to this zone prohibited to unauthorized persons?
8. Is material that was found not to be good and, therefore, to be reprocessed, checked anew?
9. Are there regulations on how defective material is to be processed?
10. Are records about defective material analyzed?

Storage, packaging, and transport
1. Does the factory make a clean and neat impression?
2. Is the material that is ready for supply clearly labeled and/or separated?
3. Do written instructions regarding packaging exist, and are they followed?
4. Is the storage satisfactorily ensured against burglary?

Customer service
1. Is there a specific procedure to process and record the recommendations and comments made by the customers?
2. Is there a specific procedure to process and record customer complaints?
3. Is an efficient communication system available to inform the customers, in case the order cannot be carried out as planned?
4. Are customer inquiries and complaints processed quickly and in detail?

In focus: Target-oriented negotiating strategy

Regardless of whether buyers are negotiating with national or international suppliers, the aim of the negotiations is always the same: best prices and top quality, together with a high supply guarantee. The »fine art« of meeting these requirements lies in determining up to what point the potential supplier is willing to »go along«, without him leaving the negotiating table in anger. Furthermore, even before the first meeting an adept buyer gathers comprehensive information about the situation in his counterpart's sector, the developments in price and demand of his products as well as the prospects of the respective industrial area. With these conditions, an even field is set for the discussions, and the buyer is in a position to refute many arguments that are so dear to suppliers, like, for example, the sharp rise in raw material prices, in a friendly, yet emphatic manner. The result: The negotiating partner loses his arguments and can therefore, as a rule, not implement his ideas.

A patent recipe for the buyer to definitely emerge victorious from the negotiations does not, however, exist. In some cases, for example, it might prove to be appropriate to come across in a particularly aggressive manner and to make forceful demands on the supplier. Such one-dimensional strategies, for the most part, however, promise only little success, at least when the aim is to build and foster a business cooperation for the long term. After all, in the course of time, the supplier will learn to be unperturbed by the buyer's aggressiveness and will not be scared away from holding on to his demands to a large extent. Exactly the same, too, is the response to other approaches, like, for example, a buyer flaunting his presumptuousness, in an attempt to show that he is actually not dependent on the supplier's products.

Therefore, it is recommended to pursue a flexible strategy that changes in the course of the negotiations. Reducing it to a common denominator, one could tritely say: One should make clear statements but still remain a »nice guy«. The first few minutes, therefore, should be used to create a pleasant atmosphere, and in the further course of the negotiations, one should come across as alternately demanding but then also as an understanding partner with whom a business cooperation could prove to be mutually beneficial. It pays, therefore, to take turns in leading the conversation, but then also to slip into the role of an attentive listener.

Do not, however, concentrate too much, during the negotiations, on getting optimal price and performance. Rather, it is recommended to make an effort to push one's own ideas of business and payment conditions through. The supplier will naturally want a corresponding trade-off for being accommodating. An announcement of a large order quantity or the possibility of building up the cooperation at a quick pace could lead to such concessions.

Finally, one could say that business negotiations are, fundamentally, comparable all over the world. However, while doing business in Asia, Eastern Europe, and Turkey, it is worth paying attention to some aspects that are different, due to the different nature and mentalities of the people in these regions. Considering the vast number of countries, international negotiations and talks are very complex, and these complexities can certainly be very comprehensively presented when viewing the country more closely. At this point in the book, we present a short overview of the countries, with particular regard to the essential characteristics and differences between companies in Western Europe and in the new sourcing countries.

Negotiations in China

Negotiating is a part of the life and culture in China. Customers haggle over prices even in department stores. This is the reason why no businessman feels affronted if he has to make price concessions. It does not, however, make any sense to force discounts. One would, at times, not like to remember these concessions while issuing the invoice. Lacking contract certainty takes every opportunity away from the customer to go against this behavior. The only option, then, is to pay the higher price as mentioned in the invoice. Negotiations are therefore, the only way to come to a reliable result. And these can be long drawn-out, because Chinese suppliers set up many side businesses and, for example, linger on with the explanation of their expansion plans. The decision-makers are exclusively the company owners and the top management. Talking with their subordinates means spending time with an activity that, ultimately, does not bring any result. If the entrepreneur were also at the negotiating table, he would perhaps very proudly present his company, in great detail, in the first phase of the talks. Those who give an impression of not being interested in these presentations, create an unfavorable negotiating position for themselves from the very outset. Hence, it is advisable to follow this ritual with a polite countenance and compliment the entrepreneurial performance. In much the same way, the entrepreneur would show you admiration, if you can come up with status symbols. Things like an impressive address in a renowned business district, or a luxury car find particular favor with Chinese businessmen. A small gift of something traditional from back home will take care of additional open-mindedness. Chinese company heads, however, would react in a hostile manner, if the negotiating partner were bent on causing him to lose face in the presence of his employees. This could be documented by the oft-intense steeliness, which entrepreneurs in China portray, when they are, as is frequently the case, accompanied by a host of employees. Besides, it could also be possible that the potential supplier initially answers with a convincing »yes«, but later does not keep his word.

Politeness and respect are essential success factors for buyers from the West. Compromises, as a rule, prove to be a good way of saving one's counterpart from the much-feared loss of face. Those who wish to build a new supplier relationship in Shanghai, however, can be assured of having to deal with business partners who react just like managers in the West. Here, visiting cards are not presented to a foreign guest in the traditional way, with both hands, but they are simply handed over with one hand in a relaxed manner. In other regions in China, this would be impossible.

Negotiations in India

Just as in China, politeness and respect are the central elements of conducting successful negotiations in India. There are, however, some differences between China and India in the way business is conducted. This can be explained by the experience of Indians with foreign trade partners, going back many centuries. In this country, hard negotiation is a tradition. Here, it is important that one really keeps a watch. Many an Indian has the almost sporting ambition to bring potential or existing business partners to highest possible concessions. It can, for example, get quite excessive, when a supplier tries to distinguish himself with his particularly good knowledge of the sector and market. If, however, he finds that the buyer is completely able to see through this and has all the latest information, then the stage is set for a successful discussion. During the negotiations, one can be sure that the price mentioned first was completely unrealistic. As a rule, there are always enormous margins. As soon as the first order has been carried out, the initial negotiating strategy gives way to a friendly, often, even family-like way of dealing. Then, there is never a dearth of topics of conversation: Many Indian managers have studied at top international universities and are well versed with the ways of the West.

Negotiations in Turkey

In the past, Turkish companies have had to come to terms with very high inflation rates. This has led to some managers thinking on a relatively short-term basis, even today. A buyer should, therefore, first present to the supplier the strategic, long-term advantages that the supplier could enjoy by getting into a supplier relationship and by establishing himself in the customer's market in the long term. When it comes to bargaining, the Turkish entrepreneurs prove to be professionals who combine the proverbial »bazaar mentality« with European coolness. Harmony, however, is one of the most important prerequisites for continuously successful business. A Turkish businessman, for example, shows his counterpart very quickly, whether he likes him or not. If the »quick test« turns out to be positive, the course is set for a successful cooperation. Nevertheless, one should not always trust every word. Whereas an Indian supplier will clearly tell you, if he is not in a position to carry out a particular performance, Turkish businessmen will first promise a lot and then possibly not be able to keep their word. It is, therefore, recommended to check whether the Turkish company can actually deliver the range of services that it offers. And, one more tip from a Turkish entrepreneur: »Do not allow yourself to be lulled by the hospitality of my fellow countrymen.«

Negotiations in Eastern Europe

The times have changed since successful negotiations with Eastern European companies depended, above all, on the ability of the Western business partners to guzzle down drinks. Companies in the EU accession countries, particularly, are similar in their dealings to Western European businesses. It, therefore, does not come across particularly well, if buyers travel into these countries with a certain amount of presumptuousness and wish to play out their alleged negotiating power there. Meanwhile, English has taken the place of Russian as the language for negotiations. Often, even German and French are spoken. Sales people in high positions conduct the talks that are characterized with great hospitality. Nevertheless, there can be ill feelings, if the Western European buyers expect completely unrealistic prices. This can definitely lead to failure of the talks, because the suppliers have excellent knowledge of the market and know their competition very closely.

The final selection of suppliers

After having gained a personal impression of the potential suppliers and their qualifications based on various criteria, it is now time to come to a final decision. It can, however, be possible that you find this final decision still difficult to make. This is not too uncommon. Often, the various relevant criteria need, once again, to be carefully weighed against each other. Decision-makers from all departments, like, for example, research and development, production, finance, and quality management, should participate in this process. While making important decisions that have strategic consequences, the top management, too, should be fundamentally included.

Despite all these efforts, if a unanimous decision can still not be reached, an additional instrument, a so-called scoring model, is available to help reach a decision. This scoring model weighs the different criteria for assessment.

	Supplier A	Supplier B	Supplier C
Quality			
• Samples	++	++	+
• Checking references	+	++	++
• Visits to suppliers	~	+	~
• etc.			
Price	++	+	~
Consignment stock	Yes (++)	No (−)	Yes (++)
Supply conditions	Ex Works (−)	DDP (++)	FOB (−)
Payment conditions	Open account (++)	Letter of credit (~)	Cash befor delivery (+)
Capacity	~	+	++
Climate for negotiations	+	~	++
etc.			

Key: ++ = very good, + = good, ~ = satisfactory, - = fair

Fig. 11 Example for final supplier comparison
Source: Kerkhoff Consulting

Procurement controlling – Basis for sustainable success in global sourcing

Consistent controlling allows the success of a strategy to be measured and reveals possible deficits. Consequently, this instrument is an integral element of sustainable, profit-oriented procurement management. This applies especially to the area of global sourcing, in which most companies have hardly gathered any experience, and are therefore particularly dependent on continuously checking and optimizing their current procurement situation. Procurement controlling in international procurement always has two dimensions. The first covers the key figures of international procurement controlling, that is, which key figures should principally be used in procurement in order to make the quality of a purchasing organization measurable. The second dimension refers to the controlling of the actual global sourcing process. When considering the process in this aspect, the criteria are subjective and are, as a rule, less valid.

Procurement controlling also allows analysis and control of the buyers' efficiency. Up until now, the employees in the purchasing departments were, if at all, assessed by their superiors with the help of criteria that were not very meaningful. Some of these criteria are the number of orders cleared or the processed order volumes. Abilities that could play a part, in a sustainable manner, in increasing the contribution of procurement in the company result are largely not considered. Employers hardly assess the talent of their buyers in the strategic area, their assertiveness, or their focused cooperation with other departments.

Principally, it can be ascertained that controlling – regardless of whether it is in nationally or internationally oriented purchasing organizations – is still a foreign word. Naturally, depending on the situation, a limit for the costs is also given. Every department, obviously, also knows the budget, and, in addition, the strategic controlling department knows the extent of the cost of materials that the profit and loss statement can bear. But real procurement controlling, often, does not exist. When our consultants, as a first step, analyze the controlling basis of the client, they find out, time and again, that absolutely nothing is planned in the purchasing department. But how can one keep a check on something that has not been planned? Controlling only functions when quantifiable goals have been set.

Nevertheless, in the framework of project implementation, we continue to experience that procurement controlling can only then be an effective tool, when some basic prerequisites are fulfilled in the company. Some of these prerequisites are:

- A key figures concept with a clear definition of the goal is present and is used.
- The company focuses exclusively on the most important areas when developing and analyzing key figures.
- Significant target figures are defined with the help of benchmarking.
- Interpretation of key figures and planning of measures for eliminating identified deficits are not carried out without previous analysis.
- Variance analysis is conducted in all participating departments, not in the purchasing department alone.

The regular control of the key figures creates a basis to put, time and again, the profit orientation of the procurement activities to the test and, in case of negative deviations, to take the necessary counter-measures without any delay.

Naturally, merely introducing a key figures system is not enough to keep a check on the entire global sourcing process. The introduction of global sourcing controlling is to be first understood as transferring the controlling that normally exists in other departments of a company to the purchasing department. At this point, it needs to be emphasized again that the introduction of these key figures does not automatically ensure the success per se of global sourcing. Correspondingly, the focus should be directed towards the global sourcing process. Every step in the global sourcing process, after all, needs to be checked – even after the contract has been awarded.

Principally, global sourcing controlling should run through five components, or testing (control) areas: (1) quality, (2) logistics, (3) costs/prices, (4) supplier(s), and (5) sourcing markets. The geographical distance leads to a completely different understanding of controlling. One can, therefore, only recommend that such internationally awarded contracts be permanently monitored. We present here a short explanation of what is to be understood under controlling in the five testing areas, and which key figures are to be implemented:

Fig. 12 Global sourcing controlling
Source: Kerkhoff Consulting

1. Quality controls

One who, for example, relies on the quality of products supplied from Asia as though they have come directly from the immediate neighborhood, is only looking at things from a short-term perspective. It is not that Asian suppliers are incapable of supplying high-quality products devoid of any defects. It is more about ensuring and keeping a check on the quality over a distance of thousands of kilometers. Adidas, for example, was successful in doing so by conducting regular tests, under their own direction, directly at the Asian production partner. It is not enough to merely rely on the controls of incoming goods. Even if it is only very simple parts that are being procured, experts from your company should keep a check on the quality at the foreign supplier's factory itself. This is the only way to ensure a certain quality, and it also more than proportionally increases the supplier's readiness to learn from his mistakes.

At this point, a natural question is, how often one should visit the supplier. To base the answer on the number of complaints alone, or on the trust placed in the supplier, would be too simplistic. There is, however, no rule of thumb. Weekly visits could be necessary in the initial phase. Once the business relationship has been established, naturally, fewer visits are sufficient. However, there is no absolute guarantee from suppliers in emerging economies. Therefore, it is necessary to carry out regular visits at quarterly intervals. Adidas, in fact, stations a quality manager permanently at the offices of the foreign partners. However, it is not always necessary to check so comprehensively. In addition to the visits, you could simply conduct surprise audits. In this way, you can keep a check on the entire production process of the supplier. De facto, one runs through a similar supplier test as already described in the checklist for the selection of a supplier, if only a brief version due to time constraints. Besides these typical questions on quality, one can also, naturally, measure the quality and quality level of a supplier with the help of concrete key figures.

Some of these are:
- rate of delay (ratio of delayed deliveries)
- rejection rate/complaint rate
- adherence to quantity stipulations
- adherence to delivery dates
- number of defectively delivered products (responsibility: manufacturer/supplier)
- number of certifications/compliance with the certifications by manufacturers/suppliers
- maintaining quality standards

2. Logistics controls

As already mentioned, logistics and its organization are very important, central elements of successful global sourcing. The logistics process is much more complex at an international level than at a national, regardless of whether one considers concrete merchandise planning, requisition note, delivery schedule, concrete deadline monitoring, invoice verification, organization of external transport, commissioning, storage in intermediate warehouses, and so on. Here, too, focused checks should be conducted. Every single step, from the time the goods leave production to the time they reach your company, should be planned and checked. Your specialized logistics partner is to be examined just as closely as the actual product supplier, whether it is in the form of unannounced visits to the port, measuring the performance of their company through key figures, or constantly comparing them with other logistics providers. Even here, you need to use all the tools of modern procurement controlling.

Key figures that can be used in the framework of logistics controlling are, for example, the following:

- inventory turnover ratio
- average period of storage
- adherence to delivery dates
- adherence to stipulations of goods
- number of defectively delivered products
  (responsibility: logistics service provider)
- number of certifications/compliance with the
  certifications by the logistics service provider
- maintaining quality standards in logistics

3. Cost/price controlling

One of the core elements of efficient controlling systems is permanently checking the costs of international procurement, as well as the prices. Only too often, the purchasing organizations rest after running through the global sourcing process. Once the companies have identified their Asian or Eastern European suppliers, they become sluggish in their work. It is quickly forgotten that these companies, too, are also in competition. Cost improvements at the supplier's end should lead to price concessions for you. Only those who constantly internationally benchmark costs and prices can carry out economical global sourcing. An example of a company from the derived timber products industry illustrates this. By changing the focus from the former European-oriented procurement to global procurement, the company could realize price advantages of up to 30 % on selected products, as early as two years ago. Even at that time, an international »price scout« was employed to exclusively conduct supplier benchmarks constantly. This is how the company succeeded in further improving its already good cost-cutting result.

Costs as well as prices can be measured:
- development of unit price of products/services
- rate of discount
- price indices for raw material intensive products
- ancillary procurement costs
- price development in the segment
- development of costs for individual components of the product (key word: value analysis)
- price development of the logistics service
- average time for payment

The cost/price controlling is especially neglected in global sourcing. Often, the buyer feels quite confident in global sourcing, purely due to the fact that he is procuring globally.

4. Supplier controlling

The cost/price controlling accompanies keeping a check on your international suppliers. Whether you make rounds of the production department, conduct comparisons within the sector, or organize strategic concept competitions even for simple parts, principally, you have a list of possibilities to constantly keep a check on your suppliers and to push for peak performance through corresponding benchmarking. Even here, the approaches of strategic procurement management, that were already mentioned, such as make or buy, simultaneous engineering, value analysis, or concept competitions, apply. In addition, it is advisable to define key figures.

Some of these are:
- number of suppliers per material group
- average quantity per order
- rate of distribution as per ABC analysis conducted on suppliers
- ratio of core and secondary suppliers to the total number of suppliers
- consolidation of suppliers and rate of building up on suppliers (ratio of suppliers removed, and ratio of alternative suppliers built up to the total number of suppliers)
- rate of accessibility of suppliers

5. Sourcing market controlling

One should, naturally, also monitor the selected sourcing market. You have already read in chapter 3, how the sourcing markets are – particularly in emerging economies – confronted with certain country-related factors of influence. Only a vigilant observation of these markets and a comprehensive sourcing market research will take care to see that regional developments do not spring a surprise on the company. Furthermore, this controlling is not just about anticipating possible crises in the country. It is also about keeping a constant check to see how long the selected sourcing market remains attractive, with consideration to all relevant cost factors.

Do not, however, make the mistake of concentrating your controlling exclusively on global sourcing. It makes sense to introduce global sourcing controlling only when it has been fundamentally laid down how procurement controlling is to be implemented, which key figures are to be planned and controlled permanently, and who bears the complete responsibility in procurement controlling.

Here, as an example, for the sake of completeness, are a few key figures that should be applied in your purchasing department:

- procurement volume
- number of suppliers

- number of articles
- number of material groups
- procurement volume per supplier/per article/per material group
- change in the procurement volume per supplier/per article/per material group
- rate of procurement (procurement volume: total turnover)
- rate of stock (average stock: total turnover)
- procurement overheads rate (procurement overheads: procurement volume)
- average value per order
- ancillary procurement costs per procurement volume
- number of orders
- number of items per order
- quantity of goods received
- costs per order
- delivery costs rate (ratio of delivery costs to procurement volume)
- lead time per order
- turnover rate, inventory ratio (ratio of material consumption to stock)
- general agreement rate (ratio of suppliers with general agreement to the total number of suppliers)
- number of interfaces with other departments
- number of employees in the purchasing department
- number of employees in the purchasing department handling operational and strategic activities
- number of suppliers per employee
- procurement volume per employee
- employee productivity
- degree of utilization of information technology
- training time per employee
- number of trade fairs visited by employees
- number of measures towards further training

Purchasing organization – Target-oriented distribution of tasks during global sourcing

Procurement management that is focused on increasing the profit, naturally, cannot function without an effective and highly qualified organization. This does not sound surprising. However, when it comes to implementing a new strategy and changing the structures, Western managers, often, fail. Many company heads do not know which concrete goals they would like to follow when structuring a new organization and, in the worst case, jump on to a new trend without any reflection. This is why, often enough, a euphorically announced entry into global sourcing meets with an abrupt end, as early as within a few months. It is precisely those who have failed at global sourcing, who are the most vehement critics of worldwide procurement. The reasons for the crash landing, nevertheless, can be found within the company itself.

This is why all those considering global sourcing should first acquaint themselves with the necessary general conditions, and define detailed and realistic goals for their project. One thing is certainly clear: The more systematically one involves oneself with the topic, the more successful the company will be. It is, therefore, advisable to comprehensively analyze, how your current purchasing organization is structured. The following case study shows how an efficient organization can have a positive impact on the company's success.

The example is of an industrial enterprise that requires ball bearings at all its five locations. By analyzing the procurement habits, it could be ascertained that all production facilities met their requirements differently. One location bought from a wholesaler, another ordered exactly the same ball bearings from the biggest supplier, and yet another ordered them from a regionally manufacturing supplier. An initiated lead-buyer-concept led to only one location being singled out to procure for the entire organization. Additionally, the procurement was consistently directed towards global sourcing. In this way, sustainable cost-cutting potential of over 15% could be realized in the short term.

This result is convincing. Before an effective purchasing organization is structured, you should determine with regard to which material group your company could be interested in global sourcing, which countries should be considered for this, whether international procurement should serve as a preliminary stage for entry into the sales market of the respective country, and what cost-cutting potential can be achieved. The financial and personnel costs for the new structures are oriented on the results of this research.

It is only then that a corresponding purchasing organization can be structured. It is, in turn, important to furnish information about your concrete ideas up to the minutest detail. You should, therefore, be able to clearly describe, among other things, which suppliers seem to be suitable as per your selection criteria.

Thus, the introduction of global sourcing poses challenges to the top management. These challenges are, often enough, underestimated and can be seldom mastered in practice without external help. More on this topic will be explained later. First, let us observe the structure of a purchasing organization.

It has already been mentioned that the conventional buyer spends the better part of his working time carrying out operational activities. This leaves hardly any time for strategic tasks, especially when one needs to adapt oneself to an entirely new procurement instrument, like global procurement. It, therefore, makes sense to distribute the operational and strategic tasks among various employees. Nevertheless, the strategists should continue to have access to operational data and should be able to stay informed about delays in delivery time, existing contracts, etc. This distribution is, however, not possible if the personnel resources are scarce. In this case, the buyers involved in operational and strategic tasks should at least be freed from the time-consuming routine tasks, as far as possible. Among other things, this functions by utilizing modern information technology, like, for example, e-procurement.

Today, strategic procurement and global sourcing demand a much higher degree of personal and technical qualification from the buyers than they did in the past. It is now not enough to just be informed about the local market and, at most, the situation in neighboring sourcing markets. A »global sourcer« should know the entire global market for his products. He should be able to sit at his computer, and, virtually with the click of a button, load all the latest developments regarding his products on his screen. Likewise, very good knowledge of foreign languages, particularly English, is a must. School-level language competency is only enough to exchange a few polite phrases with the foreign supplier. Technical and managerial questions, with which a buyer of today should be very familiar, can definitely not be discussed with this limited knowledge base. Finally, a buyer who researches globally and works with international suppliers should know how people from different nationalities respond while negotiating, and should also know what reactions to anticipate.

This is how »global sourcers« become bearers of valuable know-how, whose knowledge should be grouped together in their own competence center, at least in larger companies. When distributing tasks, it is possible to appoint employees to be responsible for certain countries or products. Combining both responsibilities can also make a lot of sense. The high qualifications of the international buyers can, therefore, be an indispensable success tool for other departments, too – from research and development and finance to production and logistics, right up to marketing and sales. No question then, that this know-how should be included in the planning and development process at a very early stage. The exact knowledge of global supplier structures and potential gives, even at this early stage, valuable information about the situation of the competition and feasible cost-cutting potential. In the area of sales, the close cooperation with the globally positioned purchasing department is, often, already a reality. Here, the employees involved in global sourcing pave the way in identifying new sales channels in the available sourcing markets and, later, even in using them.

It is, however, not enough to set up a global sourcing team only in one's own company. You should have a presence in the sourcing country through a trusted representative. It is not possible to sit at one's desk back home and carry out profit-oriented global procurement. Besides, your team will have much to do in the initial phase, in terms of adapting to the new requirements and correspondingly training themselves. International purchasing offices (IPOs) are well suited to act as representatives in a new sourcing market. Often, these service providers are not just plain traders or agents; experienced IPOs can do much more and, in this way, contribute to the success of the global sourcing strategy in a sustainable manner.

Their service spectrum includes, for example:
- solicitation of offers and offer processing
- conducting negotiations
- searching for and tending to suppliers
- offering support by providing current information on the sourcing market
- quality and progress control
- competition analyses
- guaranteeing smooth logistics
- taking over visits to authorities
- processing complaints

Naturally, not every IPO is a suitable partner. When selecting an IPO, it is, therefore, essential to take care to see that the employees come from the respective country, are experienced buyers, and have the necessary technical understanding of your product. Likewise, convincing references should also be available. In addition to these IPOs, consultants specializing in this area are also present.

As soon as the procurement volume in a country has risen to more than 30% of the total procurement volume for the year, it is advisable to establish one's own purchasing office there. By doing so, company-specific requirements can be better met. Nevertheless, setting-up and management of the office will be a further cost factor. Here, you should take into consideration that such purchasing offices largely fulfill strategic tasks, and that, correspondingly, it takes longer for the cost savings from global sourcing to exceed the capital investment. Those who dread this middle-term additional cost burden, should not, however, transfer the global sourcing tasks to existing sales branch offices in the region. Such supposed cost-cutting measures do not as a rule lead to the desired success. This is because employees engaged in sales are in most cases already over-worked with their activities, and they tend to assess markets in a completely different manner, as compared to their colleagues from the purchasing department.

In order to limit costs, many companies perhaps prefer to consider an international purchasing cooperative with businesses they are well acquainted with to achieve interesting price advantages by grouping volumes together, and, in this way, to spread the burdens of expensive global procurement. One should mention here, though, that, at least presently, the chances for success of such initiatives are relatively low. Procurement continues to be a highly sensitive area in a company, which is why everything to do with the topic is handled with extreme discretion. Besides, very often, lacking standardization of material groups prevents, in most cases, an efficient cooperation. The new generation of buyers, however, shall be more open towards cross-company cooperation and shall clear the way for collective international procurement.

One who wishes to make use of the many advantages of international procurement is bound to set up a qualified global sourcing team in one's company and be present in the sourcing market – with one's own purchasing office or through an IPO. Ademar Lins de Albuquerque, Former President, of Barclays Bank, Brazil, also holds the same opinion. »Transparency in pricing and bidding increases the stress of competition for the company concerned. However, efficient, cross-border procurement understood as Global Sourcing has the potential to offset this development and improve the business situation.« The last word of the former President of Barclays Bank: »There is still untapped potential in a professionally oriented procurement process.«

Chapter 5
Legal Aspects of Global Sourcing

Global sourcing is increasingly proving to be a matter of course for many business enterprises because of its innumerable economic advantages. In order to ensure that a business runs smoothly in the long term, and to avoid cost advantages being sapped by unforeseen expenses, a farsighted entrepreneur should pay heed to various (legal) considerations before and while concluding the contract. This will help minimize or altogether eliminate possible risks connected with international business. It is our legal duty to broadly present the potential risks on the following pages, without even slightly questioning the opportunities in global sourcing.

For simplicity, this Chapter is based on German law and the legal framework in Germany, with relevant illustrations substantiating the explanations given.

Assessment of country and debtor risk

At the outset, the German entrepreneur is advised to assess the specific risk of doing business in a particular country, and the concrete risk with regard to the debtor, while he is still looking for a suitable business partner. With regard to country risk, it is imperative to keep an eye on the political and economic risk of the country in question. The political risk could, for example, mean violent conflicts in the foreign country leading to the possible destruction or confiscation of goods, or entire industrial premises situated there. The country-specific economic risk could lie in the foreign market itself due to the unfamiliarity of the German entrepreneur with the foreign business and legal relations, mentality, business customs, language, and the like. The economically established change in currency parities too, could also be a risk in international business (cur-

Global Sourcing. Gerd Kerkhoff
Copyright © 2006 WILEY-VCH Verlag GmbH & Co. KGaA, Weinheim
ISBN: 3-527-50232-7

rency risk). Apart from the factors already mentioned, the creditworthiness of the relevant international business partner is invariably a crucial factor when evaluating the international business. Bank inquiries, credit agencies, and company figures help assess this creditworthiness.

If the buyer decides to procure goods internationally and locates a suitable supplier, after assessing the country and debtor risk, the next consideration is how the commercial business should be transacted in practice. Experience shows that many buyers conduct business as though it were with a local partner itself. Sometimes, as a result, absolutely no firm written contract is signed, or in other cases, the contract may be very limited in its scope.

Case study 1:

Buyer A has a company with head office in Germany and supplier B has his headquarters overseas. Both have verbally agreed that B will supply A in Germany a quantity X of Y goods at a particular price on a monthly basis. A wonders whether this verbal agreement signifies an effective contract, whether this agreement satisfactorily safeguards his interests, or whether further agreements are advisable from a legal perspective.

Considerations prior to the contract

The parties described in the first case study have verbally agreed to the exact object of their business as well as to the price. Depending on the law to be applied, an agreement of these minimum details could lead to a sales or supply contract coming into effect. It does, however, leave many questions unanswered that might come up when executing the contract. For instance: What happens if the supplier, contrary to the agreement, does not supply on time, or does not supply at all (key word: delay in delivery), or if the supplied goods are defective (key word: warranty)? What happens if the goods are damaged while being transported (key word: transportation risk)? Which law is applicable in case of a dispute?

In case of conflict, the legal resolution of these, and such other critical questions could prove to be long drawn-out. To steer clear of avoidable problems and the economic risk connected with them, and to form a practical and enforceable contract, a written contract is recommended in most cases.

The advantages are obvious: First, the parties to the contract are obliged to agree, right at the outset, on the most important terms and conditions of the contract. Future differences are prevented. The various risks typical of foreign trade can be reduced to a minimum, and assessed correctly by forming the contract clearly. Having a written contract also reduces problems of presenting evidence, in case of an appeal in the court regarding the arrangement between the two parties.

This brings us to the question: Which aspects should the buyer pay particular heed to while signing an international sales or supply contract, and which provisions should optimally be included in the written sales or supply contract from the point of view of the buyer? The buyer often finds himself in a conflicting position while drawing up the contract, where he has to do justice to the circumstances of the transaction of goods, interests of the contractual partner on the one hand, and protect his own interests on the other. The contract or individual clauses thereof tend to lean towards the interests of one party or the other depending on the level of awareness, negotiating skill, and balance of power among the parties to the contract. Each buyer, however, strives to formulate the clauses of the contract in such a manner so as to avoid any disadvantages for himself.

There can be significant differences in the formation of international trade contracts depending on the families of law and national legal system. Therefore, we shall restrict ourselves to those points of an international sales or supply contract that are typically the focal areas of a contractual relationship, and by following which a major part of the potential risk can be minimized. Here is an overview of this concept.

Overview: Typical provisions of an international trade contract

1. Contractual language
2. Incorporation of general terms and conditions (German abbreviation: AGB) or general conditions for purchasing
3. Basic elements of the contract
   - parties to the contract; representative, if applicable
   - subject matter of the contract
   - price
4. Agreement on choice of law
5. Delivery terms
   - Incoterms
   - individual contracts
6. Payment terms
   - agreement of payment guarantee, if applicable
7. Clause regarding allocation of risk, *as long as not already regulated by the Incoterms*
8. Duty to examine the goods and period for giving notice of defects
9. Provisions of law regarding default
   - impossibility of performance
   - delay in delivery; possible consignment stock agreement
10. Provisions for warranty
    - warranty for defects
    - warranty of title
    - statutory period of limitation
11. Non-disclosure agreement
    - possibly a penalty clause for misuse of know-how and technology, and/or violation of trademark rights
12. Duration of the contract – possibilities of termination of the contract
13. Place of jurisdiction or arbitration clause

Source: Blasius & Kollegen

Case study 2:

Buyer A from Germany and the foreign supplier B have verbally agreed, at a trade fair, to start business relations, and have until now been communicating in English. They now want to conclude a written contract. What are the aspects that they should consider in this phase of formation of the contract?

Appropriate contractual language

At the outset is the question of contractual language. The parties in our case study have already conducted business discussions in English, which opens the possibility of also writing the contract in English. There are indeed many reasons that speak in favor of choosing English as the contractual language for an international contract. Accordingly, English is decided upon when trading in many products, like, for example, raw materials. Moreover, a multitude of standardized UN directives, as well as directives of the Chamber of Commerce, Paris (e. g., Incoterms, collections, arbitral proceedings, documentary credits), and of other institutions are written in English. Finally, most credit institutes also prefer English as the primary language for contracts, and for the execution of international financial proceedings.

Offer and acceptance

The specific supply tender of the foreign supplier should contain the purchase order of the local buyer, the basic elements of an international trade contract, and as far as possible all the necessary elements for the future conclusion of the contract. The inclusion of the complete sales contract text, in the offer itself, can be of advantage to facilitate the promise of delivery of the foreign supplier and in eliminating renegotiations as far as possible.

It is necessary to keep in mind that the provisions, familiar to the German businessman, to conclude a contract by means of offer and acceptance as per German law, apply only in a modified form in most foreign legal systems.

In the case of the period of validity of the offer, in countries built on English law, it is valid to revoke an offer at any time, even if the offeror has declared himself as bound to his offer for a specific period of time.

A necessary prerequisite for effectively concluding a contract is a timely declaration of acceptance that is congruent to the offer. As per the law applicable, a delayed acceptance could be considered as a new offer, or could be entirely disregarded. Since the practice of acceptance through silence, possible as per German law, is recognized in very few other legal systems, the declaration of acceptance should be expressly stated to be on the safe side when concluding the contract.

Incorporation of general terms and conditions

General terms and conditions (AGB) should, depending on the party presenting the contract, strengthen the legal status of the buyer (general conditions for purchasing) or of the supplier (general terms of sale), and simultaneously restrict the position of the foreign contractual partner. Quite often in practice, both parties to the contract want to include their own terms in the contract (so-called reciprocal application of incorporation of terms and conditions). In such a case, the question of which conditions form a constituent part of the contract is decided by the law that shall be applicable to the particular contract.

Considering the legal position beyond one's own national borders, it can be determined that the principles to be applied to conflicting AGB terms and conditions as per German law have been established in a similar form in many other legal systems. However a uniform assessment is not possible. In the English legal system, for example, the principle of the last word as binding applies, whereas German law mutually overrules conflicting terms and conditions with regard to their conflicting parts, and thus arrives at a legal provision to be applied in the legal gap.

A German buyer may wish to include his own terms in the contract with the foreign supplier. Whether this inclusion is possible would ultimately depend on the law applicable to the contract. The relevant legal prerequisites here could vary greatly. Often, the effective inclusion of conditions for purchasing is possible if the foreign supplier agrees to the validity of the conditions for purchasing, in the case of reciprocal contractual declarations in the offer, or in the order confirmation. Another possibility is, both the parties signing a contract document in which the conditions for purchasing are explicitly mentioned. Nevertheless, it should be borne in mind that other legal systems will present further aspects for consideration. According to the law of some countries, it is necessary to expressly state and confirm the disadvantageous, previously formed clauses in a separate document, in order to effectively include terms and conditions. The law in certain American states, for example, stipulates that the disadvantageous clauses in the text are to appear in bold print.

Basic elements of a global sourcing contract

The parties to the contract should be clearly identified by name at the beginning of the contract. A need for clarification may arise if a representative is acting in place of one of the parties. If, for example, the supplier is not present at the time of concluding the contract, the buyer should check, before the conclusion of the contract, the exact authority conferred upon the representative, and whether the representative can fully act on behalf of the supplier. By doing so, the risk connected with the possibility of the representative overstepping the limits set by the supplier can be countered. In international legal relations, questions of legitimacy of the representation or allocation of the absence of intention are decided as per that national law that is ascertained with the help of the international private law of the national law that shall be applicable to the contract.

Along with the exact identification of the parties to the contract, the exact subject matter of the contract should also be clearly defined; in other words, the goods being purchased should be described as accurately as possible in terms of size, dimensions, weight, form, color, grading, quantity, quality, etc.

The third basic element of the contract is the price clause. It is beneficial to the buyer to set a fixed price, so that the risk of the cost increase of goods to be supplied falls on the exporter. In this way, possible negative consequences arising from determining an unfavorable price can be avoided. If, however, a foreign supplier is able to push his idea on the basis of his good market position, and if a price index clause that is risky for the buyer is included in the contract, then the price of the goods is determined only on delivery. Should an inflated price be set, the clause can be declared contrary to public policy, and thus be ineffective.

Minimizing risk by agreement on choice of law

While concluding an international supply contract, it is advisable, especially for the buyer, to expressly include an agreement on choice of law in the contract. By doing so, the parties to the contract establish that a specific law shall be consulted while drawing up and amending the contract. On the basis of the choice of law, if a conflict were to arise, the responsible court of law can assess the international circumstances of the case, especially for questions pertaining to allocation of risk, liability for defects, or the inclusion of terms and conditions. Of particular importance at this point is that such a choice of law exclusively refers to the contractual imposing of a legal obligation. With reference to the *in rem* rights e. g., transfer of ownership, the local law of the place where the goods are located at that point in time is applicable without exception. A contractual provision deviating from this is not possible.

In practice, both parties in contract will surely try to stipulate the familiar law of their own country as the applicable choice of law in order to use the home court advantage in forming the contract. Which party finally manages to get its idea through depends on the negotiating skills of the parties, and their market position.

If the parties do not decide upon a particular choice of law, it is up to the private international law (the so-called conflict of laws) to assess which national law shall be applicable in a particular case. According to the national conflict of laws of most countries, the law of the country having a closer connection to the contract will be prevalent for sales and supply contracts. In the absence of a contractual agreement on choice of law, during the sale of goods, in most cases, the law applicable at the ordinary place of business or at the location of the head office of the international supplier prevails. This can present a tremendous potential of risk for the buyer, who is generally not very conversant with the national law of a foreign country.

If the German buyer is in a weaker negotiating position, and is not capable of convincing the foreign supplier to accept German national law, he could press for deciding upon the unified law for cross-border trade in the form of the UN Convention on Contracts for the International Sale of Goods, if it is not already automatically applicable.

The significance on global sourcing of the UN Convention on Contracts for the International Sale of Goods

The number of countries that are now members of the UN Convention on Contracts for the International Sale of Goods (CISG) has meanwhile risen to over 60, bringing almost two-thirds of all products traded globally today under the scope of the CISG. The CISG does not, however, encompass a definitive system of sales law. The applicable national law shall complement it as required. The CISG regulates even such elementary spheres, like offer and acceptance, delivery of goods, handing over of documents, conformity of goods as per the contract, remedies for the buyer in case of breach of contract by the seller, indemnity, and interest. The sphere of application of the CISG which Germany and China for example, have entered into is either established according to the will of the parties (the so-called opting-in of the Convention on Contracts), or it is available in the prerequisites for application as stipulated in the CISG. With just a few exceptions the CISG is generally automatically applicable for international commercial purchase of goods, if the contractual countries are members of CISG, or if they follow the rules of private international law. Should the supplier come from a country that is a member of the CISG, for example, China, the stipulations of the CISG automatically apply, unless it is explicitly excluded in the contract.

The CISG also fundamentally applies to contracts for delivery of goods to be manufactured. Other rules apply, however, when the buyer himself supplies a significant part of the raw material for the goods to be manufactured. If the primary duty of the party which supplies the goods is the execution of certain tasks or services, the sphere of application is likewise not established.

Although the CISG is, in practice, classified as buyer-friendly, such generalizations should be seen critically. It is indeed true that individual provisions of the CISG as compared to corresponding provisions of German law, like the German Civil Code (BGB) and German Commercial Code (HGB) can be of advantage or disadvantage to either of the parties. Following is a broad overview of the deviations of the CISG from German civil law (HGB and BGB).

In the phase of concluding the contract, with consideration to the extent to which the offeror is bound to his offer, he can revoke his offer so long as the offeree has not yet declared his acceptance of the offer. As opposed to German law the CISG does not recognize the conclusion of a contract by a commercial letter of confirmation. With regard to the supplier's duty of delivery, the CISG differentiates whether a fulfillment of the sales contract requires the goods to be transported. In such a case, the supplier has to deliver the goods to the buyer. In other cases, the CISG, like German law requires the buyer to collect the goods from the supplier. Unlike German law, the CISG sees the duty of the buyer to pay the sales price not as an obligation to be performed at the place of business of the buyer, but rather as an obligation to be performed at the supplier's place of business. During shipment, the CISG does not pass the risk on to the buyer when the supplier transports the goods through his own people. This is also a deviation from German law.

In case of default in the form of failure to deliver goods, the buyer can demand compliance with the contract or damages due to the delay, according to the CISG. Withdrawing from the contract is possible after setting a period of grace. With respect to liability for defects, the concept of material defect is almost unknown to the CISG. The CISG however, partly grants the buyer far-reaching rights. If the failure represents a significant breach of contract then the buyer can demand for compliance in the form of a compensation delivery as well as exercise his right to withdraw from the contract. In addition, the buyer can demand a price reduction or demand damages for each material defect.

It is in the area of law of damages that one sees the most number of differences between German law, and CISG. According to CISG, claims for damages are independent of the party at fault. Additionally, claims can also be made for every objective breach of a contractual obligation, even if it is a non-essential contractual obligation. Furthermore, all conceivable contractual obligations, like the liability of default, liability to insure, duty to inform, and duty to warn are included. Claims for damages can also be raised in addition to revoking the contract. The extent of the damages is limited to an amount that is anticipated while concluding the contract. According to CISG, only monetary compensation is permitted, and not compensation in kind, when redressing claims for damages.

Case study 3:
Following the clarification of some questions regarding the conclusion of the contract, buyer A from Germany and the foreign supplier B have come to an agreement regarding the delivery of goods. They now wish to put the exact subject matter of the contract in writing, and would like to know which aspects need to be contractually regulated for the implementation of the contract, and which aspects need special consideration keeping in mind the international nature of the contractual relationship.

Performance of the supplier

International sales generally entail goods being transported over very long distances, often across many national borders. This poses the threat of extra costs and increased risk. Often, these extra costs are brought about due to the long transport distances, specific mandatory import and export conditions, or the necessity of taking out appropriate transport insurance. The risks related to the long transport distances and to the uncertainties of being granted the necessary permissions on time should be accounted for while concluding the contract. This can go a long way in ensuring the secure and smooth delivery of goods.

The parties to the contract basically have two possibilities when establishing the details of mutual obligations. The parties could include self-formulated delivery conditions in the contract. These would necessarily need to include, besides any provisions regarding packaging, insurance, etc., a provision for allocation of risk. That would mean, an agreement as to who would bear the risk of loss or damage of goods in the course of implementing the contract (key word: risk concerning performance and risk concerning the right to counter-performance).

It is important to note here that self-formulated provisions regarding delivery of goods run the risk of possibly overseeing some important aspects that might indeed need contractual regulation. In addition to that, differing business customs of the parties, as well as differing interpretations about legal terms, could lead to misunderstanding and conflict between the parties. This in turn could lead to loss of time and increased costs.

It is therefore advisable to stick to the standardized formulations, especially in international business. These model clauses, due to their international validity, present the advantage of ensuring a standardized interpretation of the terms and stipulated clauses. They also offer uniformity in many areas, like, for example, the liability of bearing the costs (e. g., custom duty, transportation costs, loading charges, and freight charges), insuring the goods, and the liability for goods that incur damage or are lost during transport. The standardized formulations are effective only when they are explicitly included in the contract.

Application of Incoterms

The latest version (updated January 1, 2000) of the so-called Incoterms (International Commercial Terms), issued by the International Chamber of Commerce, Paris, are universally recognized in foreign trade. The Incoterms consist of 13 terms, which are further grouped into four categories. The first group comprises of only one term, the E-term (Ex works), according to which the supplier delivers when he places the goods at the disposal of the buyer at the supplier's premises. According to the second group, the supplier delivers the goods to the carrier nominated by the buyer (the F-terms – FCA; FAS; FOB). As per the terms of the third group, the supplier arranges and pays for the main carriage of goods but does not bear the risk of loss or damage to the goods during transport (the C-terms – CFR; CIF; CPT; CIP). The terms of the fourth group dictate that the supplier shall bear all costs and risks until the goods arrive at the agreed destination.

The decision to adopt a particular term, from among those mentioned above depends upon the negotiating skill and market position of the contracting parties.

Disturbance of delivery

What happens if the goods are not delivered at all or if the goods are not delivered on time or if the delivered goods are not free from defects? This is a question of definite interest to the buyer. The questions touched upon here encompass the areas of German law such as the impossibility of performance, delay in delivery, warranty for defects, and warranty of title.

In an international contract, it is fundamentally left to the parties to autonomously regulate through an explicit contractual agreement that might constitute default. Most parties actively adopt this freedom in practice. Should the parties decide not to regulate the failures themselves, and should this result in a corresponding legal gap in the contract, the national law that the two parties have decided upon as the applicable law for the entire contract would fill the same. If the parties have not made an agreement as to the choice of law then the appropriate private international law would determine the law applicable in this case.

Foreign legal systems

Comparison of foreign legal systems shows that the legal systems are partly very different, with particular regard to the rights of the creditors in case of non-performance or below par performance. This is illustrated with the example of the approach to delay in delivery. According to Anglo-American law, as opposed to German or French law, a reminder or setting a period of grace is not required for the legal consequences to come into effect in case of default of payment. While German and French law, in case of default of payment, support an enforceable claim towards redemption in kind, British law only allows the aggrieved party to take legal action due to breach of contract, and to claim damages. It is only in isolated cases that British law really goes beyond the normal monetary compensation, and imposes on the debtor the obligation of fulfilling the contract. As per the applicable CISG, the buyer can, besides claiming damages, also demand delivery, or a compensation delivery, in case of defective delivery that is in violation of the contract. In the face of these differences in the legal systems from one country to the next, the German buyer would do well to keep himself informed about the legal consequences before he decides on a choice of law. By doing so, he can avoid unwanted surprises as far as possible, and ensure that the intent of the contract is maintained.

Agreements on default

It is often more difficult to meet the exact delivery dates in international business as opposed to in local business. This is why most parties to the contract lay down a period within which the goods have to reach the buyer. A consignment stock at the importer's end, particularly in case of long-term business relations, ensures the timely delivery of goods. In view of concretely laying down provisions regarding delay in delivery, it is advisable to have an agreement on the following points: Whether there is an obligation to set a period of grace, and for what length of time should such a period, if any, be fixed; whether the delivery deadline is subject to receiving all necessary permissions from the authorities; whether the liability of the supplier is limited, and whether the buyer has the right to withdraw from the contract. Moreover, in case of default, the parties very often agree to set a penalty for breach of contract, or a lump sum settlement of the damage, as the case may be. The individual national legal systems being different in this area, it should be checked whether – and if required, in which form – such an agreement conforms to the law applicable to the contract. So, for example, as per British law, a contractual penalty clause cannot be put into effect.

Warranty for defects

Of particular interest to the German buyer in the area of default is knowledge of the rights he is entitled to in case the delivered goods are defective (liability for defects). As mentioned above, maintaining individual freedom, it is entirely up to the parties to the contract to decide whether to include a self-formulated provision in the contract, to comply with a particular national law, or to simply not have an explicit agreement on this aspect. Although the parties might agree on a self-formulated clause, they are not entirely free to form it any way. They have to constantly toe the line and stay within the limits of the law applicable to the contract. It is therefore recommended, at this elementary stage of drawing up the contract, to check which law should be applicable to the contract. This is in an effort to avoid the risk, in case of a future conflict, of this provision being declared as ineffective, and hence invalid according to the law applicable to the contract.

Warranty for defects as per other legal systems

Comparing foreign legal systems shows that provisions for warranty for defects do exist in other legal systems. However, the actual rights of buyers in case of delivery of defective goods are partly very differently laid out. German law, for example, resolves questions regarding liability for defects in a fundamentally different manner as compared to Anglo-American families of law or Romanic families of law (e. g., France, Italy, and Spain).

Liability for defects as per German law grants the buyer comparatively encompassing rights. Under certain conditions, the buyer has a claim to subsequent performance, withdrawal, price reduction, and/or damages. According to German law, in a business transaction, which is regulated by the German Commercial Code, it is essential to consider the prompt duty of the buyer to examine the goods, and to give immediate notice of defects. It should, however, be noted that the parties have the autonomy to decide the actual formation of this provision on their own. If the buyer does not pay heed to his duty to examine the goods and to give immediate notice of defects, he risks losing his rights to liability for defects in favor of the supplier.

In view of the various legal consequences of liability for defects, British law differentiates between the breach of a non-essential contractual provision (warranty), and an essential contractual provision (condition). The parties to the contract can independently decide which provisions they consider essential, and which non-essential. Should the supplier breach a non-essential provision, the buyer can claim damages, independent of the party at fault, which also include damages due to defects. The goods, however, remain with the buyer. The buyer can make these claims within a period of six years by means of legal action. If, on the other hand, an essential provision is breached, the buyer can, besides claiming damages, also refuse acceptance of goods, or return the goods back to the supplier. In order to exercise this right, however, the buyer needs to make his claim to this effect at the time of acceptance of the goods.

The CISG brings liability for defects under the uniform term of breach of contract. The buyer has many rights in case the delivery of goods is contrary to the contract, that is, if the quantity, quality, or type of goods does not correspond to what has been agreed to in the contract. If there is a significant breach of contract, and if the buyer does not wish to keep the goods, he can demand a compensation delivery, or demand that the contract be revoked. If the breach of contract is not so significant, the buyer can demand rectification of the defects or a price reduction. He also has the right to claim damages, which, in case of the contract being revoked, can include the difference for a possibly higher price of a covering transaction.

Often, the German buyer attempts to bring about an agreement, in his favor, on all conceivable warranty rights that are known to him. The supplier, on the other hand, would naturally tend towards making it difficult for the buyer to claim these rights (by necessitating a written proof of the defect). In some cases, the supplier would even try to eliminate these rights for the buyer, either entirely or in part (e.g., by setting a time limit for the liability claim to be made).

The German buyer should always aim to strengthen his legal position by bringing in precise terms and conditions regarding the prerequisites, substantiation, and practical implementation of the individual warranty rights. Of particular importance here are agreements on the length of the period for giving notice of defects, and regulations on the way in which, and the time limit within which the compensation delivery should be made. It is especially useful in international business to include a clause in the contract, governing whether the buyer can undertake the necessary measures at the cost and risk of the supplier, if the supplier fails to fulfill his warranty obligations on time. An extension of the statutory period of limitation, in line with the law applicable to the contract, is also of great advantage.

Counter-performance of the buyer

An important element of the international supply contract is also the agreement on when, and in which way, the purchase price has to be paid. While negotiating the contract, both the parties will try to establish a provision in line with their individual interests. The buyer will try his best to extend the credit period as far as possible, so as not to block his capital, and to avoid cost-intensive financing. It is also in his interest to be able to check the goods for absence of defects before he pays for them. The interests of the supplier, however, are different. To avoid making an advance delivery, it would be in his interest to realize payment as early as possible. The parties to the contract need to come to an agreement regarding the exchange of services through a fair distribution of mutual risk, which comes as close as possible to a »concurrent exchange of performance«. Deviations from the same are possible, depending on the negotiating skills and position of the parties. If a special agreement is not made, then according to most legal systems, the purchase price will be due as soon as the supplier places the goods or the documents at the disposal of the buyer.

Payment terms

The parties can decide to reach a contractual agreement on the payment terms by either arranging a payment agreement, or by including documentary payment terms in the contract. The non-documentary payment terms range from »cash before delivery« (advance payment), which is the most favorable option for the exporter, to »cash down payment«, »cash on delivery«, right up to »payment net cash«, and »payment on open account«. In the last two cases, the buyer has the right to first check the goods, and where necessary, refuse payment. If the buyer is in a superior market position as compared to the supplier, he can opt for »open terms of payment«, a possibility that is very favorable for him.

Securities

In the area of documentary payment terms, there are, primarily, two options which provide an opportunity to regulate with practical relevance: letters of credit and documents against acceptance. In both cases, a financial institution is involved, which is responsible for carrying out the payment of the purchase price. The regular submission and verification of the necessary documentation of the goods is a mandatory prerequisite for the payment. The aforementioned clauses contain a special advantage; it is possible to make recourse – as with the Incoterms – to the guidelines of the International Chamber of Commerce, Paris, that are valid all over the globe. The standardized customs and practices for letters of credit, and the standardized guidelines for collections, released by the International Chamber of Commerce, Paris, contribute, in this respect, to a greater legal certainty by standardizing the interpretation, and also contribute to simplifying the process. In case of a stipulation of one of the aforementioned guidelines, care should be taken to ensure that the latest version is chosen.

Practical experience has so far shown that in cases where the business associates have not yet established trustworthy business relations, parties often make use of the letter of credit. This practice ensures that the exporter receives payment for the goods, as long as the documents submitted by the exporter are lawful letters of credit. He does not bear any liability in case of non-payment. The advantage for the importer is that he needs to deal with his bank only when lawful letters of credit have been presented.

With respect to documents against acceptance, the buyer primarily bears an increased risk. Before making the payment he only receives proof that the goods ordered have been shipped. Thus the importer is liable for the goods purchased; he can neither examine nor view the goods before payment. Since the importer's bank does not make an abstract payment promise, documents against acceptance saves, on the other hand, the risk of the exporter that the buyer will not carry out the payment and the acceptance of the goods.

Aspects to be considered in case of breach of secondary obligations

Apart from the provisions regarding the mutual exchange of principal services, the contract should also include provisions with reference to the secondary obligations of the parties to the contract. This is especially imperative when the business relations do not simply entail the supply of raw material or standardized trade goods, but when the supplier also receives an insight into the technical and economic structure of the buyer's enterprise. Such a situation causes the German buyer to fear – and justifiably so – the dishonest disclosure, or misuse of confidential information, which the foreign supplier might have obtained in the course of their business cooperation. It is recommended, in international business, to sign a non-disclosure or confidentiality agreement, because the legal protection available in international proceedings is different, and because in the framework of a non-disclosure agreement, each specific detail requiring a non-disclosure clause can be specified clearly. It is commonplace in legal systems influenced by the Anglo-American system (e. g., India) to contractually regulate every conceivable case, making it very difficult to enforce claims that are not contractually regulated. To strengthen the protection of the non-disclosure agreement, breach of the agreement should be combined with a penalty clause. Since penalty clauses are not enforceable in all legal systems, the protected party should be well informed about the national law that shall be applicable in case of a conflict, and whether the penalty clause is enforceable as per this applicable law.

Violation of intellectual property rights

In business dealings with suppliers from China, the fear of unwanted transfer of know-how, the »pinching of know-how«, is still very high. The fears are partly justified. China has indeed facilitated a formal and encompassing protection of intellectual property rights with the amendment of its patent law, concluded on August 25, 2000, well before its entry into the WTO. This is most definitely a step comparable to international standards. On the basis of effective law, it is possible to protect trademarks, business relations, and domains, and to raise claims against violators, as well as register patents and copyrights. Furthermore, the Chinese custom authorities have the right to seize goods that are suspected of being in violation of trademark rights. However, there is still a huge gap between the claims made and the reality. The buyer is, therefore, advised to safeguard himself against the violation of his intellectual property rights and the drain of his know-how, by employing technical and organizational measures. However, it is not necessary to dismiss a promising business opportunity in China only because of the possibility of a violation of intellectual property rights.

Case study 4:
Buyer A from Germany and the foreign supplier B have, in mutual agreement, laid down in their supply contract the modalities of implementing the contract. Although the buyer hopes to have laid the foundation for a successful and smooth business operation with this contract, he is uncertain whether, and if required, in which form provisions for the enforcement of law need to be added, and what other related aspects of international business he should pay heed to.

Enforcement of claims in international business

The buyer should consider the enforcement of any claims against the foreign partner as early as at the time of conclusion of the contract. The problems of enforcing claims could begin with seemingly simple questions, like the question of identity and correct name of the contractual partner, his place of residence, the head office of his company, and the ordinary place of his business. It is of great importance, while concluding the contract, to correctly identify the contractual partner by name, and not be limited to abbreviations and abstract notations. It is always more difficult to get information about the international business partner from external sources, than it is in domestic business, because public registers are often absent, or the information in them is only of declaratory significance. The early friendly phase of initiating and concluding the contract could, therefore, be used to source, from the business partner itself, all the information that might be necessary for enforcing claims in the future.

Contractual guarantees

Guarantees for the enforcement of claims, like, for example, payment or bank guarantees and insurance, could be laid down in the contract to avoid the parties having to turn to the court for settlement. These possibilities are generally only implemented in the export business, but are suitable even for international procurement.

Out-of-court settlement of disputes

The parties to the contract would be keen to settle a dispute out of court, before they take the legal path. Before he spends worthwhile time and money on long, drawn-out correspondence and business visits, the claimant should be aware of when his claim shall become barred by the statute of limitations as per the applicable law, and, if required, how the lapse of the statute of limitations can be halted or delayed. The legal systems of many countries can have some very surprising statutes of limitations.

Legal disputes

If a legal dispute becomes inevitable, it is worthwhile to try to carry out the legal proceedings in one's own country. The jurisdiction of the German court can either be agreed upon contractually, or be decided upon due to the international competency of German courts. From the point of view of compulsory enforcement, however, it makes sense to carry out the legal proceedings against the foreign partner abroad. This is particularly true if the domestic judgment towards compulsory enforcement abroad would not obtain recognition, or perhaps obtain recognition only with great difficulty. Other factors that speak in favor of carrying out the proceedings abroad are: the likely duration of the proceedings, the cost of the proceedings, the accessibility of evidence, and the question of on which national law the appealed court shall have to base its verdict. In this regard, it is recommended to enquire with an internationally active law firm, or with a German-speaking lawyer in the particular foreign country about the conditions of undertaking legal proceedings.

Enforcement of German judgments abroad

Since March 1, 2002, based on the regulation »Brussels I«, German judgments are enforceable in Europe. This regulation almost completely replaces the EuGVÜ (European Convention on Jurisdiction and the Enforcement of Judgments), concluded on September 27, 1968, which, however, is still in force with respect to Denmark and some other overseas member states. In relations with Iceland, Norway, Poland, and Switzerland, the LugÜ (Lugano Convention on Jurisdiction and the Enforcement of Judgments in Civil and Commercial Matters), signed on September 16, 1988, is followed. For countries outside Europe, bilateral Conventions on Recognition and Enforcement of Judgments are – partly – applicable. It is advisable to be well informed about the possibility of enforcement of the judgment abroad before getting into a time and cost-intensive legal dispute. Should the judgment gained locally not be enforceable abroad, the agreement on the place of jurisdiction for deciding legal disputes will be worthless.

Arbitral proceedings

It is often recommended to solve legal disputes through arbitral proceedings, because of the restrictions present in enforcing local judgments overseas, and vice versa. An arbitration agreement is, however, a prerequisite. With amendments in the arbitral proceedings from December 22, 1997, German legislation has entirely re-written the regulations of arbitral proceedings in the Code of Civil Procedure (ZPO), with effect from January 1, 1999. Furthermore, the regulations of arbitral proceedings of the International Chamber of Commerce, Paris, which enjoy global recognition, have been amended effective January 1, 1998.

It is mandatory for the so-called arbitration contract to be in written form. It regulates the allocation of an arbitral court, and specifies the details of the rules applicable for the proceedings. The arbitral award is effective as a legally binding judgment for the parties (§ 1055 Para. 6 ZPO); the judgment, therefore, cannot be further contested through legal means. This is a disadvantage for the unsuccessful party, because he cannot appeal to a higher authority to examine the case, and possibly overrule the arbitral award. Should the unsuccessful party not fulfill the arbitral award, then the judgment, which had been declared as enforceable, shall be carried out as compulsory enforcement. An ordinary court, however, needs to declare the enforcement of the judgment. The ordinary court does not examine the correctness of the arbitration, rather only whether essential mistakes were committed in the course of arbitral proceedings.

Advantages of arbitration

For international business, the advantage of arbitration is that it offers the possibility of declaring both local arbitral awards as enforceable overseas, and foreign arbitral awards as enforceable locally, as per the »Convention of June 16, 1958, on the Recognition and Enforcement of Foreign Arbitral Awards«, to be able to carry out compulsory enforcement. As at February 2005, this Convention had been ratified by 135 member states. Among these are Germany, and some other countries that are paramount to global sourcing – China, India, Turkey, Poland, and the Czech Republic.

Important international institutions too, deal with arbitration. Noteworthy among these is the International Chamber of Commerce (ICC) in Paris. Some Arbitration Rules that were last amended on January 1, 1998, are applicable for the arbitration of the ICC. Also of particular significance are the UNCITRAL (The United Nations Commission on International Trade Law) Arbitration Rules, and the Arbitration Rules of the German Institution of Arbitration e. V. (DIS).

Most of the Arbitration Rules require both the parties to name one arbitrator each, and these arbitrators agree to a third arbitrator, who acts as the chairman, so that there are an odd number of arbitrators in the court. By choosing their arbitrators, the parties can exercise a certain amount of control over the arbitral proceedings, and thereby ascertain that the court is competently occupied. A further advantage of the arbitral proceedings is that the process does not take place publicly, and that the relations between the parties are not revealed. There is, however, a disadvantage: the remuneration of the arbitrators is on an hourly basis due to their expert knowledge, and this hourly rate is comparable to that of well-paid lawyers. Arbitral proceedings, therefore, turn out to be more expensive than ordinary court proceedings. The high cost is, however, compensated by the speedy proceedings, and by restricting to one authority having charge of the proceedings.

It is, therefore, worthwhile to be informed not just about the ordinary jurisdiction of the particular country from which procurement shall take place, but also about its arbitration. Countries with a long tradition of trade often have a well functioning process of arbitration. That point is illustrated here with the example of China.

Arbitration with the example of China

Arbitration in China is now regulated on the basis of the Arbitration Law of the People's Republic of China that came into force on September 1, 1995. The »Middle Kingdom« has two institutions for settling international legal disputes: since 1954, the China International Economic and Trade Arbitration Commission (CIETAC) for commercial disputes, and since 1956, the China Maritime Arbitration Commission (CMAC) for maritime disputes. The CIETAC is one of the busiest arbitration commissions worldwide. The reason is partly because the Commission itself, and not one of its constituted arbitral courts, decides whether an effective arbitration agreement has been presented. Arbitrators can only be authorized by the Arbitration Commission, and this authorization too, needs to be renewed every three years. The list of arbitrators contains several well-known personalities from various professions, among them many foreigners, including some Germans. These arbitrators have to follow certain canons of professional ethics. As per the Chinese Arbitration Law, arbitrators are required to perform their duties impartially, and to abide by the law. The official language of the proceedings is Chinese (Mandarin). If the proceedings are carried out in Chinese, the Arbitration Commission can make arrangements for an interpreter, if required, and can also arrange for the presentation of English or Chinese translation of the submitted documents. This is quite common for legal proceedings involving foreign parties.

Course of arbitral proceedings

The course of arbitral proceedings, including the oral hearing, corresponds to the legal proceedings in continental Europe. The parties have to first present the facts of the case, and the issues that are in dispute, in writing. Arbitration Rules are not stipulated. An investigation by the office does not take place. The arbitral court is, however, authorized to conduct an investigation and gather evidence, as far as it deems necessary. The oral hearing is based on the written submission made by the parties, and is, therefore, comparatively short; it normally does not exceed one day. The parties have to prove the facts on which their claim and their defense are supported. Unlike in England, the hearing of evidence is not in a form of cross-examination. Arbitral proceedings often end in a settlement, especially when financial claims are involved. Just as in Germany, whether and when this takes place in reality depends largely on the persuasive arguments supplied by the arbitrator. With regard to the arbitral award, the arbitral court can award the successful party the costs incurred by him in the arbitral proceedings.

In summary: The German business partner should consider, as early as at the time of formation of the contract, where the specific legal risks of business relations lie, and how he can most favorably enforce his claims. A well thought-out and enforceable contract helps in avoiding risks, and deters the contractual partner, at the outset, from violating the contract.

Chapter 6
How Global Sourcing Promotes Profitable Growth and Increases the Shareholder Value

European CEOs are known as excellent restructuring specialists all over the world. In the area of growth management, however, top managers from the country do not fare so well. According to a study of *Manager Magazin* from April 2005 French and British company heads prove to be essentially much more efficient in this area. For them, profitable growth is directly connected with entering global markets. For the top managers of France and Great Britain, however, being internationally present does not merely mean capturing foreign sales markets, but also procuring abroad. In Europe, there are still only few who recognize global sourcing as strategic growth management. And not all stock corporations are aware that global procurement positively influences the shareholder value.

Medium-sized companies do not need to worry about shareholder value, because most of these companies are privately owned. They turn to their own resources when financing the company, or, if required, they take long-term bank loans. Many of them still carry out procurement in the traditional way: from longstanding suppliers from around their region. By doing so, these entrepreneurs give away the chance of stabilizing in a sustained manner or clearly increasing their profits. In addition, by not entering into global sourcing at the right time, they forego the opportunity of adapting to the ever-intensifying price wars in the framework of rapidly increasing international competition.

On the following pages, we shall present the impact of global sourcing on the profit situation of a company. In addition, you will see how cross-border procurement can contribute to a good rating result based on the Basel II guidelines, equity regulations regarding bank lending, and how it can influence cooperation with investors. Private equity investors are presented with the influence of

Global Sourcing. Gerd Kerkhoff
Copyright © 2006 WILEY-VCH Verlag GmbH & Co. KGaA, Weinheim
ISBN: 3-527-50232-7

global sourcing in increasing the value of their portfolio of companies.

How does global sourcing influence the rating based on the Basel II guidelines?

In the future, procuring credit will become more difficult for hosts of small and medium-sized companies, because, according to the Basel II guidelines, banks and thrift institutions will be forced to subject borrowers to a quantitative and qualitative rating. Those who do not fare well in this test will have to deal with higher credit costs and, in the worst case, have to fear their house banks »axing their funds«. Some credit institutes are already working according to these strict allocation guidelines. This procedure is especially hard for medium-sized companies, because their lean equity ratios force them to go in for a high degree of external financing. In comparison to an average equity of 20 % in Germany, medium-sized companies in the US have an equity ratio of 45 %. The situation is similar in Spain and Great Britain, where the equity ratio is about 40 %.

Until now, credit institutes referred to past developments while conducting credit assessments and above all, analyzed financial ratios. Ratings based on the Basel II guidelines, however incorporate a future-oriented consideration. Here, the main criteria in focus are the company's capacity to register profits in order to be able to pay back the credits, the strengths and qualifications of the management, and the position that the potential borrower enjoys among his competition. Additionally, the efficiency of the purchasing department is also checked in this assessment. Here, the factors to be assessed are the organization of the procurement management, its position in the company, the allocation of personnel, and the international orientation.

Professionally conducted global sourcing massively contributes to being able to present the company to banks as an innovative and continuously profitable enterprise. The income/expenditure ratio can thus be clearly improved through cross-border procurement. On the other hand, one should use global sourcing to optimize the »debt-equity ratio«, (i. e. the relation of debt capital to equity capital), which is a decisive factor for banks and thrift institutions. After all, every percentage point that is saved through international procurement has a direct bearing on the company result and with it, increases the equity ratio. The outcome: The rating result is positively influenced, and the credit costs decrease or at least remain the same. The following example illustrates how a comprehensively implemented global sourcing positively influences the profit and loss statement and thus the balance sheet of a company. For the sake of simplicity, we shall exclusively look at items that cannot be capitalized, which means that negotiable balance sheet items on the asset side (fixed assets) are not considered.

All figures in thousand euros	Without global sourcing effect	With global sourcing effect	Global sourcing effect in %
Sales	500,000	500,000	
./. Manufacturing costs	332,500	299,250	10
Gross profit on sales	167,500	200,750	
./. Research and development costs	40,000	38,000	5
./. Sales costs	75,000	75,000	
./. General administration costs	20,000	17,000	15
Miscellaneous operating income	5,000	5,000	
./. Miscellaneous operating expenses	10,000	8,500	15
Distribution of ownership	2,500	2,500	
Income from financial assets	5,000	5,000	
./. Interest	800	792	1
Operating profit	34,200	73,958	
./. Tax on income and profit	8,892	8,892	
Extraordinary profit/loss	500	500	
Net profit	25,808	65,566	
Profit brought forward from the previous year	8,500	8,500	
./. Share of other partners in the profit	1,000	1,000	
./. Appropriation to the revenue reserve	2,000	2,000	
Balance sheet profit	31,308	71,066	

g. 13 Effect on EBIT from global sourcing
ource: Kerkhoff Consulting

How global sourcing additionally illuminates the profit and loss statement

Already strategic domestic procurement massively contributes to optimizing the profit and loss statement (P&L) of a company. These positive effects can be further increased with global sourcing. The manner in which global procurement impacts the essential elements of the P&L is illustrated with the following observations.

On the previous pages, we have already presented how a lot of companies do not use their commitment in global sourcing markets to merely generate sustainable cost-cutting potential. Very often, lucrative sales markets are created out of sourcing markets without much additional expense. For example, purchasing offices owned by the company that are located in the sourcing market, help in identifying potential for their company's products and in preparing a successful market entry. Global sourcing can thus indirectly contribute to positively influencing the turnover in a sustainable manner. The rating agency Standard & Poor's, in fact, awards geographical turnover diversification plus points in its ratings and, by doing so, paves the way for favorable financing conditions. The entry into a new international market is not possible without experienced sales experts. Nevertheless, the sales costs can be clearly reduced due to the available market knowledge, the framework of legal conditions and the already existing networks.

The manufacturing costs are largely determined by the material usage. However, as already explained, not all materials used are suitable for international procurement. With particular regard to quality and transportation costs, it is important to exactly differentiate which products can actually be procured globally. In order to do so, every company head has to define his individual decision criteria. From our long years of experience we can safely say that, when intensively considering all the products and services to be procured, a much larger share comes under »capable of being sourced globally«, than most of our clients assume. It is almost always worth it. The success can often, in fact, be exponential, if not just individual parts are procured abroad, but also orders of complete assemblies are awarded to corresponding international suppliers in the context of so-called make or buy decisions. Naturally, it is not about »quick wins« in the sense of short-term cost-saving effects. Here, it is about middle-term supplier relationships that are marked by a high share of development.

The costs of research and development, too, are influenced by cross-border procurement. However, we increasingly come across the prejudice among our clients that foreign suppliers, when compared to well-known local suppliers, cannot reliably take over or accompany the research and development process. Judgments like »copyists« or »cheapjack« are not too uncommon – too unfair, in my opinion. Our experiences, after all, substantiate the technological capability of suppliers from low-wage countries. My recent talks in Asia with a manufacturer of control boards for consumer electronics reflect a completely different self-image of the suppliers located there. In this company, one goes as far as rejecting inquiries from foreign companies that exclusively aim at procuring parts which have already been designed, in large numbers at the lowest possible prices. They see themselves more as competent contact partners of the design and development departments of the potential buyer. Many renowned branded companies of the international consumer electronics industry are already on their list of customers. Recently, the company, in fact, won an international design prize. I was proudly taken through sprawling development departments, where excellently qualified technicians and engineers work.

A comparison of the hourly wages between graduate engineers in Europe and their equally qualified counterparts in Asia very quickly shows that attractive cost-cutting potential can be found in the area of research and development. In addition, the current data transfer technology makes it completely irrelevant, whether the development experts work at the company back home or in a far-off country. The illustrated example is representative of a whole list of similar impressions that we collected in the areas of tool construction, packaging, and light industry.

At first, one may hardly believe that global sourcing can also result in interesting cost-cutting effects for general administrative costs. Think, for example, of services in the IT sector that are procured from corresponding consultants today. The expert comes, as a rule, to the company, and he charges for the travel costs and the number of hours of work he puts in at the company. In the future, thanks to the Internet, these costs will be reduced tremendously – and for 24-hour service in return. Meanwhile, there are enough BPO providers who carry out IT-enabled services for large organizations like banks and insurance companies. In this area too, the high personnel costs of German employees are confronted by the comparatively much lower wages of employees in India thus punishing those companies that allow such cost-cutting potential to go untapped. Besides, fears that relocating a telephone hotline abroad would negatively impact customer contact for reasons like language difficulties can quickly be put to rest by simply paying a visit to the company. The employees in the BPOs visited by us were, in fact, even in a position to speak to customers from different regions of Great Britain in their specific accents.

Finally, there are the miscellaneous operational expenses. This area, as a rule, is not even in the focus of cost-cutting activities for national procurement. Consequently, procuring from international markets is seldom taken into consideration. Very often, ordering such products or services bypasses even the purchasing department and is done directly by the respective departments. A big mistake because here especially, one can find many starting points for global sourcing. We know an example of a renowned European stock corporation, where the printing of the company's annual reports devours hundreds of thousands of euros year after year. When planning the lead-time correspondingly and considering the logistical framework of general conditions, a much cheaper printing shop in the Czech Republic or Poland could definitely be suitable as service provider. Another example is advertising material or the so-called promotional gifts like cigarette lighters, umbrellas, caps, or pocket calculators. Here too, there are good opportunities to source such products in the corresponding sourcing markets with essentially more favorable conditions, rather than simply falling back to the wholesaler from the neighborhood.

Global sourcing as a growth booster

Achieving growth is the strategic objective of every company. Implementing these growth objectives is, however, largely influenced by external general conditions in practice. Often enough, constant cost pressure from the customers the accompanying price decline on the sales side, rising competition as a result of increasing globalization and many stagnating markets are the factors that oppose the targets set by the company. High production costs due to continuously rising ancillary labor costs, too, negatively impact the prices of European products. The complexity of growth strategies therefore requires considering many partial strategies that fundamentally affect all areas of the company. International procurement and production offer a way out of a possible cost trap. Global sourcing can thus become an integral element of an efficient growth management. The company growth drives procurement into a new arena – the sourcing markets that are yet to be developed.

What exactly is growth management?

Fundamentally, the company growth depends on three factors:

1. Successful interaction with the environment of the company, like, for example, sourcing and sales markets, suppliers, customers, etc.
2. Resources available in the company, like financial resources, production capacity, employees
3. Knowledge, skills, and ambition for growth of the entrepreneur or the entrepreneurial team

According to the Product/Market Matrix by Igor Ansoff, the »father of strategic management«, four different kinds of growth strategies can be implemented. Starting from the current position of the company, growth can first be achieved along with market penetration by enhancing the ongoing business. The strategy of market development aims at opening new sales areas or target groups for the available product range. Often both methods are implemented with aggressive price wars on the sales side and, therefore they inevitably increase the pressure on procurement. The purchasing department, then, has to look for new ways, and this search almost »automatically« leads to global sourcing. A third strategy is the consistent introduction of new, innovative products. This process requires innovative strength, together with the early identification of new trends. Here too, the purchasing department can help to a large extent. After all, this department should be best informed about the latest technological trends because it is the constant contact partner of the supplier. The most challenging form of growth is diversification, that is, the development of new products and their sales in hitherto unknown countries. If the purchasing department, in the context of global sourcing, gains experience in potential new markets then it can serve as an important informant to the sales department on matters like the competitive situation or market structures.

Finally, growth management aims at managing the constantly increasing complexity which accompanies the presented forms of company growth, in an appropriate and target-oriented manner. In order to do so, the companies should gradually develop and build their skills in the various operational areas. This is particularly applicable to procurement. The internal structures and resources should be reorganized to keep pace with the increasing size of the company and with the internationalization that normally accompanies growth.

Growth management tries to find answers to these questions:
- Why should the company grow?
- How can the growth planning be structured?
- What challenges does growth present to the company?
- What are the critical growth barriers in the development of the company?
- How does one recognize the necessity for change at an early stage, and what possibilities for action are available?
- How is growth potential recognized, assessed, and realized?

How Global Sourcing Promotes Profitable Growth
and Increases the Shareholder Value

Global sourcing and internal growth management

With regard to the possibilities of realizing internal growth, that is, market penetration or market development through global sourcing, one should first analyze the general conditions of the sales markets from the point of view of procurement. Broadly summarized, this is what the current situation looks like: The price pressure is consistently rising due to increasing globalization and is, in this way, becoming a decisive factor in the definition of future growth strategies. The pressure on the suppliers to carry out further services in the areas of logistics, development, and assembly with regard to the actual end product, and to simultaneously guarantee a constant pricing structure, is increasing. This means that internal growth is realistic only when the companies face up to the customers' requirements. Optimizing procurement through differentiated, international market development is, therefore, a basic prerequisite in order to develop a sustainable foundation for internal growth. How acute the impact of such activities can be is underlined by the fact that, today, the area of materials, often, amounts to over 50% of the total costs. Moreover, in this area cost-cutting effects are realized much quicker. Strategic decisions in the production department that could lead to product segmentation or relocation of the production location, on the other hand, demand much longer time for preparation and implementation.

The potential sourcing market is expanding even further in the course of globalization. This development will continue as long as technology and wage differentials exist between regions, and, at the same time, transaction and transportation costs decline. If a company wishes to grow, the buyers consistently have to find the right supply sources all over the globe. Solely cooperating with local or regional suppliers is not enough to survive in this price-intensive competition.

Global sourcing and external growth management

External growth is frequently associated with acquisitions of companies, both locally and abroad. First of all, this brings about an additional coexistence of individual purchasing organizations of different strategic business units which have to be connected to each other. Regularly, however, determinants can emerge, for example, a geographically defined supplier market or a technologically definable material group, on the basis of which the purchasing department can be oriented. This kind of growth represents ideal combinations, which, in the short term, enable the purchasing department to realize cost-cutting potential even abroad. This is possible because, due to the acquisition of other companies, corresponding market knowledge is already available and can be used across the company. In these cases, through acquisition the additional procurement volumes extend to technology and to such markets that are equally or closely connected with the current volume, that is, with the volume of the buying company. Approaches like grouping of suppliers, standardization, or technological benchmarking across all international locations help overcome these challenges, without making it necessary for the purchasing department to acquire completely new technological or market-related know-how. To profit from this available knowledge, the function of an on-site buyer, for example, is extended to additional factories or regions.

Certain cost-cutting potential can, naturally, be realized only after undertaking corresponding preliminary work, like, for example, developing a platform strategy. Automobile manufacturers that employ a common mechanical basis for several different series of models increasingly use this system. Reduction in the variations of the end product can, likewise, contribute to reducing the costs. The areas of sales and development create the product-strategic and technical prerequisites. The assessment and application of such potentials is the responsibility of the purchasing department. In this regard, the department should organizationally reposition itself between the market and the internal departments in case of modified general conditions of the company.

Global sourcing as a value enhancement instrument for private equity houses

In most of the Western world, private equity is on everyone's lips. Although ten years ago, the sector was considered largely questionable, with the image of the breaking-up of companies attached to it, today it has restored its reputation. On an average, the European Private Equity and Venture Capital Association (BVKEVCA) calculates corporate venturing investments of about 1.2 billion euros since 2002. The development in the last twelve years, alone, illustrates that the demand for equity capital is pointing to a growth market.

Between 1991 and 2004, the equity market has grown at an average rate of 15% per year. We can assume that the sector will develop just as dynamically in the future. The driving force behind these continuous upward trends, primarily, is the high capital holding of institutional investors, who also look for attractive investment opportunities for the future. Additionally, there are many other reasons that lead to accepting equity partners, and, in this way, positively influence the business in private equity houses. As already described, it is about the requirement to show the banks a higher equity ratio according to the Basel II guidelines, for example. In addition, the forthcoming follow-up regulations for medium-sized companies will, likewise, lead to intensified usage of external equity. In such cases, one can think of possible management buy-outs and their financing. Besides, one should also consider that the demand for growth capital, as already explained, does not have to be unilaterally financed from the banks. Thus, in this area, too, a demand arises which will primarily profit the equity partners.

Recently, so-called mega deals are making the headlines. These are, however, not included in the statistics of the BVK. Nevertheless, there are enough examples of such transactions. The US financial investor KKR, for example, did not simply buy out the chemical division Dynamit Nobel from mg AG (formerly Metallgesellschaft). In a »secondary deal«, the Americans also took over the automobile workshop chain Autoteile Unger from a British holding company. Cognis, the former chemical division of Henkel, went to a financial consortium of the investment houses Permira, Goldman Sachs, and

Schroders. Regardless of whether they are medium-sized financial transactions or mega deals, all financial investors follow the same goal: they want to sell their stock at a much higher price or shareholder value in three to seven years.

How does a financial investor increase the value of a company? This is, de facto, the key question for the entire sector. Upon looking more closely, we see that often private equity houses concentrate exclusively on »financial engineering measures«, that is, the development and implementation of creative financing models. Otherwise, the project leader responsible for the holding company returns to the role of controller. Unfortunately, in this business one frequently oversees the fact that only added value is offered when strategy management is carried out. If one additionally clarifies that the value of a company will increase only through concrete measures, the question that is then raised is whether the typical conduct of the private equity investor is not too shortsighted.

Fundamentally, after coming on board, the private equity investor should run through four process steps in order to actually be able to sell the company at a higher value in the end. In each of these phases, procurement in general and global sourcing in particular should receive special consideration.

Here is an explanation of the four steps: In the first step, the question »Where does the company stand today?« is jointly answered with the first and second-level management – despite the results of the due diligence, that is, the careful examination of the strengths and weaknesses of the company to be acquired. The result is a detailed assessment of the current position of all business areas, of corresponding potential, and is a comprehensive analysis of the strengths and weaknesses, known as »SWOT analysis«, which is based on the key figures of the balance sheet, P&L, and other earnings-related indices like ROI (return on investment) or ROCE (return on capital employed). The comprehensive integration of all results alone permits the exact assessment of the current position of the company and the derivation of strategic paths for growth. Thus, the first step can be understood as an effective completion of the due diligence and is a sort of »kick-off event« to determine future potential. An exact examination of the current purchasing organization is one of the integral elements of the first process step. A private equity house should not solely restrict itself to questions of whether the purchasing department is operative in a traditional manner or is managed through modern procurement methods, whether the purchasing organization is working efficiently, or whether the existing suppliers are monitored and analyzed regularly. In addition, it is also important to learn how far the procured services are systematically checked to find out whether they can be procured globally. This check reveals the strengths and weaknesses of the purchasing department and identifies procurement-related value leverages.

In the second step, one determines where the company should be in the next three to five years, in order to have become really successful. Questions of penetration in existing markets, market or product development, or, in fact, diversification into new areas are discussed, and their effects on the company result are estimated. Here, too, it is important to establish the future purchasing organization. One should determine which products or services can be procured nationally and which internationally. Accordingly, an organizational adjustment should follow, and the national purchasing organization should be supplemented with international organizational units.

Step three gives information about how the company can reach its comprehensive growth objective. It is exactly at this point that the actual concept of value enhancement is determined. Should the company grow internally, that is, with its own strength and without diluting the culture, or should it grow externally through acquisitions? A detailed strategy sets out the strategic growth objectives for the next three to five years. With regard to the purchasing organization, one should once again define here how the determined procurement targets are to be reached. The entire procurement management is oriented nationally and internationally, with respect to the organization of its development and operation.

Finally, in the fourth step, one identifies how successfully the company functions. It is exactly measured how professionally conducted procurement management, the clear orientation of the global sourcing activities, impacts the value of the company. Ultimately, thus, one »controls« the chosen path. An integral element of this check is international procurement controlling. With this, the circle is completed with a return to step one. Weaknesses can be corrected, strengths consistently developed.

The four steps illustrate how easily management of value enhancement can be implemented. Only those who stick to this action plan will be able to generate value in a sustainable manner. In order to achieve this, global sourcing should be integrated in all phases. This instrument holds a very special charm for financial investors: they can increase the value of their stock solely by professionalizing the entire procurement management. Here is an example of the same: Let us assume that a company, at the time of entry of a private equity house, registers a turnover of 100 million euros, a gross profit of 60 million euros, and an EBIT (earnings before interest and taxes) of 10 million euros. The financial investor assesses the company based on an EBIT multiple of five with an enterprise value (shareholder value including debt) of 50 million euros. After five years, the turnover remains constant at 100 million euros, because markets did not develop as planned. Despite the stagnation, with global sourcing the equity investor could reduce the cost of materials by 10 million euros. The result: The EBIT rose to 20 million euros. Subsequently, while selling, the assessment of the company was based on the exact same EBIT multiple. Correspondingly, the enterprise value rose to 100 million euros. This corresponds to an annual increase in value of 19 %, without the turnover needing or having to be expanded.

This simple, pragmatic example illustrates the positive impact of professional international procurement management on the private equity commitment. Financial investors should, therefore, use global sourcing as an instrument to increase the value of their stock, in a sustainable manner, and, with that, ensure its worthwhile sale.

Global sourcing in the case of listed companies – positive effects on the shareholder value

Shareholder value continues to be one of the hot topics of the economy. Although critics repeatedly point at the short-term nature of shareholder value management, listed companies should, naturally, not dispense with it and should rather increase the value of the stocks to keep the stockholders satisfied. And this in a sustainable manner. Global sourcing contributes to supporting this process. The focused reduction of cost of materials or the outsourcing of entire sub-processes is a good basis to optimize all the key figures relevant to shareholder value. In this way, relocating services to low-wage countries, for example, can have a positive impact on the development of the stock price. The German Axa AG, a subsidiary of the French insurance company Axa S. A., focuses on the same, as well. According to a report of the leading German newspaper *FAZ* from April 2005, the company is planning to slash 680 jobs all over Germany in the next two years. A part of these, in the areas of audit and information technology, will be outsourced to India or Latvia. This relocation will influence the stock price in the long term. Even the private stockholders and institutional investors will see that the Axa group is strategically managing its costs in order to remain competitive in the long term.

Only very few companies have recognized the benefit of active global sourcing towards improving the value of their company and, thus, towards correspondingly increasing the attraction for investors. If one combs through a list of major companies and analyzes which company has a central executive board for procurement, one would hardly find any. The large automobile concerns are, however, exceptions and have corresponding departments. Gisbert Langheim, former head of purchasing at Skoda, wonders about this when he says, »Even today, most of the large companies still confuse procurement with merely beating down the price quoted by suppliers. That procurement is, indeed, a strategic task of creating a long-term association with the suppliers is, however, seen only by a few.«

All financial key figures that are related to the cost of materials can, de facto, be improved through global sourcing, and thus, impact the shareholder value. Naturally, not just listed companies, but all companies can profit from this.

The equity ratio describes the relation between equity and total capital. The more the equity capital that is available, the better is the financial strength, as a rule, and the company can operate with less dependence on debt capital investors. The composition of equity capital follows the allocation of the annual net profit in the balance sheet. In short, every percentage point that can be saved during procurement of materials within the scope of a global sourcing strategy, which, among other things, is reflected in the P&L under cost of materials, increases the net profit. With that, it also increases the equity ratio when the entire amount is allocated in the balance sheet. Critics will rightly object that should the equity capital be more expensive than the debt capital, then too high an equity ratio would strain the return on capital employed. Naturally, this is correct; however, a lower cost of materials increases the net profit. At this point, it is advisable to let the financial experts fix the appropriate amount of the equity capital.

A higher net profit is, naturally, closely linked to an increased gross profit margin. This key figure reveals the percentage of sales that is available to the company as gross profit. Trade, in this case, refers to the trade margin. The historical development of the gross profit margin shows how the procurement prices of a company have developed. This also makes it an indicator of how professionally procurement is carried out. In the course of our consulting projects, we frequently see marked improvements in the gross profit margins.

The cost of materials ratio is directly connected to the gross profit margin. It represents the share of cost of materials in the total costs and, thus, describes the cost-effectiveness of material usage. If the cost of materials ratio decreases, while the turnover remains constant or increases, then this development suggests an increase in the productivity of material usage – often, the result of favorable procurement prices due to global sourcing. As a rule, once the cost of materials is among the major expense items, this key figure reflects the efficiency of the company to a large extent.

One of the most important indicators for measuring the economic success of a company is the realized EBIT margin. It represents the percentage of operating profit of a company before interest, tax, and financial results. This key figure, thus, gives information about the earning power of the company. Professionally and correctly carried out global sourcing has a positive effect on the EBIT margin due to the reduced costs. However, the procurement of some material groups does not directly improve the result, because such material groups cannot be displayed as investments on the

How Global Sourcing Promotes Profitable Growth
and Increases the Shareholder Value

balance sheet. One such group is intensive expenses that influence the taxable profit base only through the amount of depreciation. In these cases, when faced with corresponding queries, we take only the liquidity into consideration and explain that a lower burden of liquidity exists, because of the favorable procurement of fixed assets. The free cash flow (calculated as annual net profit + depreciation – investments), that is, the resources that are freely available to the company, increases significantly. Therefore, this key figure is, in fact, positively influenced from two sides. The EBIT is the basis for the calculation of free cash flow. As already described, it increases directly as a result of professional global sourcing. To calculate the free cash flow, the investments are subtracted from the EBIT. If one assumes that global sourcing does not just lead to a higher EBIT, but also reduces the necessary resources for investments, then the free cash flow indirectly increases twice as much.

Recently, aside from the well-known key figures of profitability, like return on equity, the operating margin or return on investment (ROI) are also calculated as key figures for shareholder value. All these values improve through global sourcing. An increasingly often-used assessment criterion is return on capital employed (ROCE). It compares the EBIT against the capital employed for a period and displays the earning power of the total capital. This key figure is, however, viewed critically in practice, because capital costs are not taken into consideration and because exclusively financial accounting figures are integrated in the calculations. Despite this, you will still find the realized ROCE in almost every annual report of large listed companies. Rightly so, because it illustrates the purely operating success. In addition, an adjustment of profit and assets which do not contribute to the actual operational process, takes place. If we integrate our global sourcing approach in the ROCE, this key figure, too, will greatly improve. Finally, as mentioned, the EBIT and, with it, even the ROCE (calculated as EBIT / [fixed assets + working capital]) improve through global sourcing.

The various key figures listed here can only indicate, as an example, how actively and correctly carried out global sourcing increases the shareholder value. All result-related data get influenced in a positive manner. Every CEO or chairman of the executive board should be aware of the positive effects of global sourcing on the world of his key figures. Analysts, institutional investors, and stockholders will be grateful to him.

Index

Global Sourcing. Gerd Kerkhoff
Copyright © 2006 WILEY-VCH Verlag GmbH & Co. KGaA, Weinheim
ISBN: 3-527-50232-7